MW01092476

MYSTERY AND THE
ADOPTED CHILD

Renée Henning

(2018)

Printed in the United States of America

First edition

Book cover design by Gratzer Graphics LLC

ISBN-13: 978-1987551433

ISBN-10: 1987551435

I am an adoptive mother and an adoptive aunt, including to young adults from Russia, Asia, and Latin America. I dedicate this book to them and to the memory of my beloved husband.

CONTENTS

PROLOGUE

All children are a mystery to their parents to some extent. Yet adoptive parents face many more questions than birth parents about a child's past and heredity. This book of articles written over twenty-four years discusses people adopted from around the world and their sometimes surprising behavior.

So why did an infant need to bang his head repeatedly to get to sleep? See the article on sleep for the reason. What food-related problem resulted in a four-year-old with a sensational throwing arm? See the food article for the answer. Why did a boy insist on a belt and undergarments so tight that they left welts on his body? Similarly, why was a teenager from an unloving birth family sexually promiscuous--despite not liking sex? See the article on touching for the rationale, which turned out to be the same in both cases.

Clues often point to trouble in the child's past as the cause of his odd behavior. For example, the preschooler in the siblings article who ate crumbs off the floor and garbage had, prior to adoption, been neglected and hospitalized for malnutrition. Mystery and the Adopted Child looks at pre-adoption experiences, subsequent events, and how adoptive parents solved certain problems.

In short, adoptees tend to be fascinating and complex individuals who sometimes mystify their families and others. This book will give readers answers to various mysteries relating to adoption. In a way, the book is also a love letter to adopted youngsters everywhere.

SLEEP AND THE ADOPTED CHILD[1]

Often it is hard for new adoptive parents to learn much about their child's pre-adoption life and current emotional state. This can be particularly true if he came from a foreign country, joined them before learning to talk, or experienced an unspeakable trauma. Initially, the child's sleeping patterns may mystify his new family. However, some adoptive parents have uncovered clues to the past life and current state by observing those patterns.

A family adopted a one-year-old boy named Jack[2] from Latin America. At the time of the adoption, he was hyperactive, malnourished, and the product of foster and institutional care.

Like many hyperactive children, Jack was very active even in his sleep. He could not stay covered by a blanket for five minutes. His sleeping positions kept changing, but he always appeared to be on the defensive while asleep.

Furthermore, Jack could not doze off without a bottle, which he clutched during the night. He had entered his last orphanage chubby and emerged badly malnourished. For various reasons, his parents suspect that the older children in the orphanage were stealing the milk of the younger ones like Jack.

---

[1] "Sleep" was first published in 1992.

[2] All names in this article were changed to protect the children's privacy.

One night the boy's mother made the mistake of trying to add to his comfort by gently loosening his grip on the bottle as he slept. Jack immediately woke up sobbing. He thought his mother was trying to steal his milk.

In the first three months in his adoptive home, Jack woke up repeatedly during the night crying for another bottle. Often he would go through five bottles of baby formula in one night, with no adverse effect on his appetite the next day.

Jack's parents were able to solve the problem of the child's getting cold from lack of a blanket by buying blanket sleepers (sometimes called sleeper suits) of winter weight. The parents had a more difficult decision to make with regard to the bottle.

The medical and dental professions do not favor allowing children to fall asleep sucking a bottle. While Jack's pediatrician believed in giving an adopted child unlimited food in the first year after the adoption, he advised against crib bottles because of the increased risk of an ear infection. The family dentist also recommended against crib bottles, because of the risk of tooth decay.

The parents had to balance the physical concerns against the emotional concerns. Like many adopted children, Jack did not arrive with a teddy bear or other favorite toy. His primary comfort was the bottle. The parents decided to work first on providing emotional security and to postpone bottle weaning until later. They wanted him to learn quickly two rules of the house: (1) children here do not go hungry; and (2) children here do not have to be on guard in their sleep.

Approximately four months after Jack's arrival, his parents saw one of their happiest sights ever. They walked into the nursery and found him wholly relaxed in his sleep. The toddler was not holding his bottle, which was tossed aside in a corner of the crib. He was flat on his back with both arms lying above his head. In his yellow sleeper suit, he looked like a fuzzy duckling totally at peace. Jack had finally learned the rules of the house.

Some children, including infants, provide useful clues to their new adoptive parents through other sleeping patterns. One baby named Robin could not go to sleep without head banging. At bedtime, it looked as if he was knocking himself into a stupor against his pillow. Prior to his adoption at age eight months, he had survived six moves and six changes in his primary caretaker.

Robin's alarmed parents consulted their pediatrician, among other sources, about the head banging. They learned that some children denied adequate stimulation get into the head-banging pattern or a comparable rocking pattern as a way to make themselves sleep. (Some other children develop this sleep-inducing routine despite ample stimulation.) The parents suspect that their son, like many other babies drawn from an institutional or foster-care setting, had been left for long periods alone and unstimulated in his crib. Because the head banging was not hurting Robin, the parents were advised to let him continue the practice.

The boy also exhibited another sleeping pattern shared by many newly adopted children. He slept far more than is usual for a child of his age. Sometimes he slept so much that there was time for only two feedings that day. Concerned about his slow weight gain, Robin's parents consulted their pediatrician. It turns out that withdrawal through sleep is the method used by many adopted children to cope with the stress of a radical change of life or the mourning for parts of the old life. The pediatrician advised the family to let Robin sleep as much as he wished. According to the pediatrician, the baby eventually would need far less sleep.

For months, Robin was basically interested only in sleeping, eating, and being held. It was as if he was "down a quart" on hugs. Once his mother held him on her lap for two hours until she had to get up; Robin himself showed no interest in escaping.

After living in his new home for about five months, Robin began needing a lot less sleep. He slept a normal number of hours for a child of his age. He also proceeded to grow nearly four inches in a four-month period.

In retrospect, Robin's parents think that all the hugs paid off. In their view, the boy no longer felt the need to hide in sleep. Robin had finally learned that he had found a permanent family.

Many adopted children are afraid to be alone in a darkened room. They may avoid sleep for fear of a monster hiding in the dark. This sleeping problem is, of course, also found in many birth children and can often be solved by a night light.

However, the problem may be aggravated in adopted

children by the fact that many of them (particularly those born in foreign countries, raised in orphanages, or from large birth families) are accustomed to sharing a room with other people. Such children are not used to being left alone in the dark and, if young, are likely to prefer having a roommate.

In such a situation, one adoptive family with enough bedrooms to give everybody one has doubled up the two small boys in a room. Both youngsters clearly prefer sharing a bedroom to having separate rooms. The parents plan to give each child his own room when he is older and wants more privacy.

Some of the sleep-related problems of adopted children are far more serious and may require therapy. For example, one family adopted an older American girl named Ginger, with the knowledge that she had previously experienced physical abuse. The new parents discovered that Ginger had trouble sleeping and was scared of the dark. It took the parents a while to find out the explanation, based on an additional trauma from her past life. She turned out to be afraid of the dark because a child molester used to come to her at night. Sadly, for some adopted children like Ginger, the monster hiding in the dark was real.

From observing, hearing about, and reading about the sleeping patterns of various adopted children, I have concluded that the patterns sometimes can provide clues to the child's past life and to his current state. For new parents of these children, I have a message. Time (often about six months for the transition period), love, patience, and a sense of humor can help you and your child through.

For our adopted children everywhere I also have a message. May sweet dreams come to you!

PLAY AND THE ADOPTED CHILD[3]

It has been said that play is the work of a child. A child can learn about nurturing by playing with a doll, about gravity by playing with a ball, and about social skills by playing with a friend. Play is so significant that pediatricians use it to measure a child's development (e.g., a youngster who can build a tower with blocks and perform certain other play functions before a certain age is deemed developmentally advanced). Thus, it can mystify or shock adoptive parents if, as often happens, their newly adopted child lags far behind his peers in sports and other play activities. The parents may begin to fear that he is of poor intellect or even mentally handicapped. However, there generally are more benign explanations for the apparent developmental delay, as illustrated by the story of Tam.[4]

More than twenty years ago a French family, consisting of two parents, a teenager, and a three-year-old boy, adopted Tam, a twelve-year-old Vietnamese boy who had experienced considerable hardship. The parents assumed he would be a companion to the teenager and would be enchanted with all his new, age-appropriate toys. Instead, Tam preferred to play with the three-year-old and the latter's toys. For a while he exhibited no interest in his peers or in

---

[3] "Play" was first published in 1994.

[4] All names in this article are pseudonyms to preserve privacy.

his own toys. The family began to fear that he was mentally disabled.

However, over time Tam grew bored with his younger sibling's toys and friends. He wanted to play with the toys of a five-year-old, then of a somewhat older child, and then of a somewhat older child. He eventually worked his way up to the toys of his age level, passing through each stage much faster than would the average child. Tam also became interested in playing with children of his age. Ultimately, it was determined that the boy, far from being intellectually disabled, had an above-average IQ.

The parents have their own explanations for what happened. In their view, Tam, who had had few toys as a child, had to work his way through the different stages of playthings before he could be comfortable with age-appropriate toys. As for Tam's initial preference for the companionship of three-year-olds, they spoke French closer to his beginner's level than did his older sibling and were at his level of unsophistication about French life.

It is quite common for newly adopted children who are older, come from a foreign country, or arrive from an institutional or foster-care setting to exhibit developmental delays in sports or other play activities. Often the explanation is lack of opportunity, not lack of capability, as illustrated by the story of Jack.

The boy, who was born in Latin America, was the product of foster and institutional care. By the time of his adoption as a one-year-old, he had spent considerable time penned up in a crib, from which he had made repeated, unsuccessful efforts to escape.

When Jack came to the United States, he appeared to be behind his peers in some respects. For example, during his first few trips to a playground, he seemed to know nothing about the swings and slides and to be timid of them. (Given the likelihood he had never seen a playground before, this is not surprising.) The child also appeared to know little about some age-appropriate toys. Handed a push toy, he did not know how to use it, even after some demonstrations. Instead, he ran merrily around in circles with the toy sometimes upright, sometimes upside down, sometimes in front of him, and sometimes behind him.

However, by the age of three Jack had caught up with his peers and surpassed most of them. To find him in a playground, you had to look for a boy at the top of the jungle gym or a boy on the swing yelling, "Higher! Higher!" He is a star athlete in his play school. In addition, according to the school director, Jack is very intelligent and, in one area, a genius.

It turns out that Jack was a natural athlete and smart all along. He simply had been cooped up too much in a crib and lacked exposure to the American playthings on which his developmental level was being tested. Given the opportunity, he, like many other adopted children, seized it.

A foreign-born child may appear to be hopeless at a sport like baseball. However, this should not be construed as meaning that he is unathletic and behind his peers. It may turn out that he excels in a favored sport of his native land, as illustrated by the story of Angela.

The girl, who was adopted at age eleven from a Brazilian orphanage, seemed backward by American standards in various respects. However, promptly after arriving in the United States, she became the star of her American soccer league. In her native Brazil, where the playing level is higher, she had not been considered remarkable. Angela's unathletic father, who could not have expected to produce such a child biologically, is surprised and delighted by his daughter's athletic stardom.

Often newly adopted older children, particularly those adopted internationally, are teased by their American peers because they cannot play a particular sport, such as tennis, or cannot ride a bicycle. Once again, the explanation for the apparent backwardness tends to be lack of opportunity (and lack of a loving home), not lack of capability. To learn how to play tennis requires a tennis court and racket, to which the foreign-born child is unlikely to have had access. To learn how to ride a bike requires a bike, which he probably did not have.

It may be comforting to reflect on what would happen if the positions of the foreign-born child being teased and the American-born child doing the teasing were reversed, so that the latter was carried off by a new family to a foreign land. It is likely that in many cultures the transplanted American would be viewed as backward, because of his lack of knowledge of community expectations and community games. Indeed, I know of cases where a child of immigrants was brought up to meet American standards and was then considered backward by relatives in the immigrants' native land.

In any event, from what I have observed and read, there is plenty of good news for adoptive parents of many seemingly backward children. First and best, many, like Tam, do catch up with their peers, and many even surpass their peers.

Second, the adopted child who is introduced to a sport or plaything later than other children is likely to learn how to play the sport or use the plaything faster than normal for a beginner (because of being older and physically and mentally more advanced than the typical beginner). Tam is one of many examples of this phenomenon.

Third, the adoptee is likely to arrive with some talents he might not have developed had he been born to his new family. For example, Jack, who had to "make do" with regard to toys before he came to the United States, has been described by a play-school teacher as being able to play creatively with anything. Not having been brought up with rigid notions of what is or is not a toy, he became an innovative child. Similarly, Angela, the eleven-year-old from Brazil, would probably not have been a star soccer player had she been born in the United States.

Fourth, there is especially good news for the many adoptive parents who regret having missed the pre-adoption portion of their child's youth. Often the parents get to observe and participate in developmental stages they thought they had missed entirely. For example, Tam's parents saw him develop in effect from a three-year-old to a teenager in a compressed period.

Finally, there is a special joy reserved for the adoptive parents of many seemingly backward children. This mixture of pride and satisfaction comes from taking someone who, by American standards, was developmentally backward, giving him love and opportunities, and then watching that once backward child shine!

So laugh and play, adopted youngsters everywhere. For all of the many developmental gains you have already made, we are already proud of you.

<u>MYSTERY AND THE ADOPTED CHILD[5]</u>

All children are a mystery to their parents to some extent. For a child born to the parents, the explanation for a particular mystery often becomes clear upon reflection. To make sense of his unusual personality, behavior, or fears, the parent may only have to recall a relative's personality quirks or an earlier experience that frightened the child. In contrast, in the case of adopted children, the adoptive parents may not know the child's birth relatives or the scary experience. Thus, adoptive parents face more mysteries than birth parents about a child's past and about the extent to which heredity is influencing behavior in the present.

Even children adopted as infants present mysteries. One example is Robin,[6] a product of institutional and foster care in Central America. He survived six moves and six changes in his primary caretaker prior to being adopted at age eight months.

Initially, Robin's adoptive parents were mystified by his sleeping and eating patterns. From a time predating the adoption, he could not go to sleep without head banging. At bedtime, it looked as if he was knocking himself into a stupor against his pillow. Furthermore, when his parents first met him months before the adoption, he resisted being fed in

---

[5] "Mystery" was first published in 1994.

[6] The names of all children in this article were changed to protect their privacy.

any position but horizontal. It quickly became clear that Robin was accustomed to eating lying down.

Robin's parents turned to their pediatrician and other sources for an explanation. They learned that some children who have been neglected get into the head-banging routine or a comparable rocking pattern as a way to make themselves sleep. Many babies in institutions are left alone and unstimulated in a crib for much of the day. In some of the institutions, infants are fed lying down with the bottle "propped" in place (so even at mealtime they are not being held).

Robin is now two-and-a-half-years old. Given his history of multiple primary caretakers, psychologists might have predicted an inability to bond, among other attachment disorders. In fact, the boy is very attached to his mother. In the winter, you may find him walking behind her holding on to her coat. In the summer, you may find him following on tiptoe, hanging on to her swimsuit. Robin, once asked by a play-school teacher to name something that made him happy, smiled and said, "Mommy."

With regard to sleep-related patterns, Robin still bangs his head to get to sleep. However, the duration and force of the head banging have diminished. He has also developed another sleep-related habit. Just before lights-off time, he loads up his bed with books and toys. Some nights Robin's bed is so crowded that the mesh side rails are bulging, and his mother has to clear a little space for him to fit.

Robin's parents have their own explanation, based on

diverse facts, for some of his behavior. In their opinion, Robin, like many other babies drawn from an institutional or foster-care setting, had been left for long periods alone and neglected in his crib. However, questions remain. What is the explanation for Robin's need for physical contact with his mother and for the bulging bed rails? As for the hanging on, is this simply an affectionate child? Or is this a child who, having finally found a mother, is reluctant to let go of her? As for the bulging bed rails, is this a child with an amusing eccentricity? Or is this a child with a half-buried memory of being penned up in a crib with nothing to do, day after lonely day? Robin's parents will never know.

Another boy, Jack, exhibits a combination of toughness and sensitivity found in many adopted children. He experienced hard times before being adopted as a toddler from a foreign orphanage with a mortality rate allegedly over 50%. To the surprise of his new parents, he virtually never cried when hurt but was always the first person to console someone crying. It was Jack who tried to comfort a stranger with Down syndrome who was hysterical. It was Jack who rushed forward to hug the knees of a wino drinking on a park bench. And it was Jack who was the only child in his play-school class willing to play with a handicapped classmate. According to the boy's teacher, there is more love in Jack's little finger than in the whole body of his classmates.

Besides being highly compassionate (and popular), Jack is a good judge of character. He loves almost everyone. Yet, in the year after he joined his new parents, there were three people he rejected on sight. The first person, encountered by chance on the street, was an employee of Jack's orphanage. The second was a sadist whose child-rearing methods included inducing her son to burn himself on a hot stove and with matches. The third was a lady known throughout the neighborhood for her good deeds. This woman, who was surprised at Jack's rejection (because most children like her), later was found to be responsible for some despicable acts.

Was Jack born with a high threshold for pain, or did he learn at an early age that crying got him nothing? Was he always inherently loving and a good judge of character, or did he learn through suffering to be compassionate and to recognize cruel people on sight? Or is the answer to these questions both genetics and environment? It is impossible to know for sure.

In any event, many children adopted from institutions expect little sympathy yet are sympathetic to others. They know what it feels like to be ignored and unwanted. In contrast, too many biological children who were the center of their loving parents' attention end up self-centered rather than loving. In the case of Jack, the source of his toughness on himself and his compassion for others will remain a mystery forever.

Sometimes mysteries can be solved through persistence, as illustrated by the story of Sam. The boy was adopted from Korea at age five. His birth mother had both loved and neglected him, sometimes leaving him home alone and scared for hours.

Sam presented a mystery to his adoptive parents from the start. Even after his arrival in the United States, he insisted on wearing clothing so tight that it left welts on his slender body. Given clothes of the proper size, he would fasten his belt and twist his undergarments so hard that he must have been in pain.

Sam's new mother was determined to find out why her beloved son was hurting himself. It took more than a year and considerable persistence, but she eventually found a professional who could unravel the mystery. It turns out that the too-tight clothing was an attempt by a child desperately in need of hugs to hug himself.

It is fortunate that little Sam ended up where he did. If there is anyone who can make up for his hug deprivation, it is his wonderful, warm-hearted mother.

Despite the stories of Robin, Jack, and Sam, most people adopting little children are unlikely to encounter mysteries stemming from shocking or traumatic events. Many of the mysteries posed by adoptees are funny, charming, or sweet.

Nonetheless, people should not adopt if they are unwilling to accept mystery in their child. While some mysteries can be solved by meeting with a birth parent, an interim caretaker, or a professional, other mysteries cannot. People troubled by the thought of an insolvable mystery should remember that, even with biological offspring, not all unusual behavior can be attributed to a specific past event or a particular relative. Children are full of surprises.

In fact, adoptive parents have an advantage over

biological parents with regard to these surprises. As newspaper columnist Ellen Goodman pointed out, adoptive parents are more willing to accept a child for the unique individual he is, because they know he is not their clone. Instead of assuming that he is just like them in predilections, athletic abilities, artistic talents, skills, intelligence, and temperament, adoptive parents set out to know the child as himself--and in the process let him be himself. Thus, according to Ms. Goodman, adoptive parents start out in the parenting business one step ahead of everyone else.

Furthermore, as time goes by, an adopted child may present fewer mysteries to his parents, because of their shared past. Moreover, people who consider it desirable and fun to remain a bit mysterious to their spouse may come to appreciate a touch of mystery in their child.

So, to our adopted children everywhere, I propose a toast. To the mystery and wonder of you!

PREJUDICE AND THE ADOPTED CHILD[7]

Prejudice takes many forms. Some companies discriminate against older women in hiring (which is age and sex discrimination). Some people distrust all young black men (which is age, sex, and race discrimination). Yet another prejudice targets adopted children and strikes <u>because</u> they are adoptees.

This article focuses on one form of anti-adoptee prejudice, the reaction of some people to an adopted child's birth certificate age. The bias is against children, concerning their age, and because they are adopted (which is age and adoption-status discrimination and, sometimes, race, ethnicity, or nationality discrimination).

This prejudice can be seen in the refusal of some people to accept that an adopted child's birth certificate is right. They may try to explain away the adoptee's achievements by spreading the rumor that he is older than his actual age. The stories of Tim, Paulo, and Jesse[8] illustrate the prejudice.

Tim

Tim was adopted from Asia at age five. For various reasons, there is no doubt that the birth date on his birth certificate is correct.

Soon after arriving in the United States, the boy was the

---

[7] "Prejudice" was first published in 1994.

[8] For privacy reasons, every name in this article was changed.

guest of honor at a family reunion hosted by his aunt Ellen. To the surprise of his new relatives, he proved to be the best-mannered child at the party. After he left with his parents, other guests were marveling aloud at how handsome, tall, and polite he was.

Then the hostess, who has a son a little younger than Tim, offered her opinion. According to her, no five-year-old could be that polite; because of Tim's good manners, as well as his height, he could not possibly be that age.

At first glance, talking against a young guest after his departure may appear merely unkind. However, in this case it is also prejudiced. The Aunt Ellens of this world, meeting for the first time an unusually polite child, would never deny his age publicly--unless that was an adopted child. Moreover, Aunt Ellen's opinion can be very damaging. If listeners believe her, a boy who at first appeared handsome, tall, and very polite for his age is suddenly just a pretty face. In addition, any future outstanding achievements by the boy are suspect (i.e., the achievements may be deemed proof that Aunt Ellen was right, rather than as remarkable accomplishments for the child's age). In short, by casting doubt on Tim's age, Aunt Ellen was casting doubt on his contemporaneous and future accomplishments.

The basis for this prejudice against adopted children appeared initially to be a mystery. However, from what I have since observed, the prejudice stems from one or more of the following biased views:

1. My biological child cannot possibly be shown up

by another parent's adopted child (i.e., a matter of pride, jealousy, etc.);

2. Adoptees are all backward and all behind birth children with regard to anything good;

3. Only the U.S. has good record-keeping, so any foreign record, including a birth certificate, is suspect;

4. Foreigners and minority-group children are short, so if an adopted child in either category is tall for his age, that is not his age; and

5. Foreigners and people who are not 100% Caucasian are genetically inferior to an American-born Caucasian child, so if a foreign-born or minority adoptee excels for his age, that cannot be his age.

Evidently, one or more of these biases motivate some people to try, without solid proof and despite contrary evidence, to persuade friends or relatives not to believe an adoptee's birth certificate. Unfortunately for Tim, who turned out to be a bright, delightful boy, he may have encountered all five biases.

Paulo

It is not only children adopted at an older age who are the victims of anti-adoptee prejudice concerning age. Even infants can be targeted, as illustrated by the story of Paulo.

Recently, two colleagues were discussing adoption. One of them, Rachel, has no children. Rachel mentioned that her neighbor had a baby, Paulo, adopted from Brazil. She said that he was big. Then she added casually, "I don't think he can be his age, because he's very advanced." Surely Rachel would not have disputed Paulo's age had he been born to the neighbor before Rachel met them (i.e., if he had not been adopted).

Jesse

An adopted child does not have to be tall or precocious to be the victim of anti-adoptee prejudice regarding age. Children who are below average in height or who have some developmental delays are also targeted, as shown by the story of Jesse.

Jesse was an infant in a foreign land when his adoptive parents first saw his photograph, and they met him before he could walk. Initially, he was delayed on various fronts. However, even as a toddler, he was, according to his play school's staff, very intelligent and athletic. Jesse at age four was judged by staff and by five-year-old classmates to be the best athlete in his school.

Before Jesse joined his new parents, another boy, Billy, had been the only grandchild in the parents' extended family. The whole family believed Billy to be an incredible star. Then Jesse arrived. He was six months younger and much smaller than his cousin Billy and, unlike Billy, had experienced hard times. Nevertheless, while Jesse was still a tot, it became obvious that he was more advanced in athletic ability and certain mental skills than Billy.

That started the trouble from Aunt Joyce. Aunt Joyce is Billy's mother and Jesse's aunt. She is pleasant, capable, and against American citizenship for many U.S.-born people (including all children of a foreign-born adoptee). Aunt Joyce, after observing Jesse outshine Billy in some respects at family parties, concluded that Jesse had to be substantially older than he really is and that she should tell all the relatives (except for his parents).

When Jesse was two, Aunt Joyce, discussing his accomplishments, told the relatives, "No two-year-old can do that." What she actually meant was that no adopted, immigrant two-year-old can do that. Yet the boy really was that age.

One of the relatives tipped off Jesse's mother to Aunt Joyce's rumormongering. The mother was hurt but did nothing to stop Aunt Joyce. In part because Jesse in some ways acted young for his age, the mother assumed that kind-hearted relatives could not possibly believe the lies. However, she did predict to her husband that Aunt Joyce, to prove that Jesse was really older, would be checking him when he turned five to see if he had lost any baby teeth.

Just after Jesse turned five, there was a family reunion. Promptly after greeting his mother, Aunt Joyce brought up the subject of teeth. After mentioning that five-and-a-half-year-old Billy had lost a few baby teeth, she said, "Jesse must already have lost a lot of teeth."

In reply, Jesse's mother called her son over. With glee, she had him open his mouth to reveal--a full set of baby teeth.

Jesse is now six years old. His mother is delighted to report that he still has all of his baby teeth. She predicts that the next big test will come when Jesse turns twelve. About then Aunt Joyce should start checking his chin hoping to see a beard!

<u>The Adverse Impact of Anti-Adoptee</u>
<u>Prejudice Concerning Age</u>

At first glance, anti-adoptee prejudice regarding age may seem a rather innocuous form of prejudice. In fact, it can really harm an adopted child and his family.

Among other things, this prejudice has the potential of undercutting the child's strengths and highlighting his weaknesses in the eyes of people closest to him--relatives and family friends. If people believe an adopted child to be older than he is, they will be unlikely to consider him advanced in any way for his age. For example, he will get little credit for learning to ride a bicycle right after turning five if relatives believe him to be seven. In congratulating the child on his bike riding, relatives who consider him five may think "good"; relatives who consider him seven may think "finally." Perhaps worse, this prejudice works to magnify the adoptee's shortcomings. For skills in which he is a little behind for his birth certificate age, relatives who believe him to be older may think, "What's wrong with him that at his [imagined] age he <u>still</u> can't do that?"

In short, this prejudice robs an adopted child of credit for his achievements and can make him appear hopelessly backward in skills for which he is a little backward for his birth certificate age.

The prejudice also places the adopted child in a no-win

situation. The more he shows himself to be very intelligent and multi-talented, the more likely some people are to believe that his talents corroborate the rumor. Only by acting backward and unworthy of praise can the advanced child hope to convince those people that he truly is his age.

Furthermore, the prejudice can damage the adoptive family's ties with relatives and friends. It can help poison an adoptive parent's relationship with someone the parent holds dear. Upon discovering anti-adoptee prejudice in relatives or friends, adoptive parents experience mixed emotions. For example, Jesse's mother says she was amused, furious, hurt, and sad (on behalf of her son, her husband, and herself) to discover Aunt Joyce's reaction to little Jesse's hard-won achievements. Some adoptive parents report feeling shocked and betrayed.

This does not mean that the prejudiced person has no right to express an opinion. Everyone has the right to express his opinion, including the opinion that a child is older than his birth certificate age. In the case of anti-adoptee prejudice, the problem is the motives for that opinion and for broadcasting that opinion (e.g., prejudice against adoptees and other prejudices), and the underhanded way most rumormongers spread that opinion (tell almost anyone but the adoptive parents). Thus, the rumormonger should be free to express his opinion, and the adoptive parents should be free to express their opinion of the rumormonger's motivations and sneakiness.

In some cases, the adoptive parents do not find out about

the rumormongering. This tends to be because well-meaning relatives or friends who heard the rumor had hoped to spare the parents' feelings or to preserve family harmony.

If a parent does learn of anti-adoptee prejudice against his child, he can, like Jesse's mother, elect to do nothing. However, the woman turned out to be wrong in assuming that no relative would believe Aunt Joyce's rumor or remember it. The rumor can have a lasting impact, as she discovered in an encounter with a distant male relative more than three years after the rumormongering had occurred.

Indeed, the rumormongering itself may recur repeatedly over the years. Aunt Ellen, the relative of polite Tim, eventually informed his parents of her doubts about his birth certificate. After the conversation, she professed herself satisfied that the certificate had not been forged. Nonetheless, as of a week ago (i.e., several years later), Aunt Ellen, though citing different "proof," was still spreading the story that Tim is older than his birth certificate age.

Suggestions for Dealing with Anti-Adoptee Prejudice Regarding Age

If an adoptive parent does choose to fight back against this prejudice, he should consider ways to do so that may avoid a family feud. Here are five suggestions for dealing with the prejudice.

First, in the case of abandoned children, there may be some question about the child's exact age. The adoptive parent should tell about the abandonment and any doubts about the age only on a "need-to-know" basis (e.g., to the child's pediatrician). The parent should remember that in some cases where the age of an adoptee appeared uncertain, it was subsequently discovered that he was <u>younger</u> than his birth certificate age.

Second, where the prejudice exists, the parent may wish to mention, infrequently, physical characteristics indicating a younger age (<u>e.g.</u>, the youngster still has his baby teeth or still retains a toddler shape) in talking to people who heard the gossip. The parent should <u>not</u> point out how backward his child is in learning to read, ride a bike, or reach other milestones. The gossipmonger has already done plenty to undermine that child; the child does not need his parent's undercutting him, too.

Third, the parent may wish to raise the subject of anti-adoptee prejudice with or without naming names (<u>e.g.</u>, if the parent suspects rumormongering, without admitting to the suspicion). For example, the parent can say in the presence of some relatives that: (1) he read about the prejudice and its basis; (2) he feels sorry for adoptive families who had to put up with a relative talking against an adopted child behind the adoptive family's back; and (3) he is glad to think that those present are not like that.

If a relative then volunteers the information that there was talk within the family against the child, the parent can express his hurt and disappointment and request an end to the rumormongering. Through this approach, the parent may succeed in shaming the rumormonger into silence (since, even if that person is absent, the story may get back to him) or in opening other relatives' eyes to the rumormonger's real motivations.

Fourth, the parent can give relatives, including the rumormonger, a copy of this article. Then everyone can draw his own conclusions about the rumormonger's motivations!

Fifth, the parent may wish to talk with the source of the rumor. For example, the parent can point out to the gossipmonger that he knows far more about his child's background than that person; he would appreciate it if, in the interest of family harmony, that person would stop spreading gossip about the child. Alternatively, the parent can say that he was hurt to learn of the rumor and of the person's talking against his child behind his back; the parent would appreciate it if in the future that person would come to him with any perceived problem concerning his child.

During the conversation with the prejudiced relative or friend, the parent should not go into details about his reasons for knowing his child's birth certificate to be accurate. Nor should he accept being cross-examined on his child's background. (The only proof the rumormonger is likely to accept is that the parent witnessed the child's birth.) Moreover, the parent should not reveal the name of his informant, because it will only cause trouble for that person. Finally, the parent should keep the discussion short.

Whatever a parent decides to do to combat false rumors about his child's age, he should remember that there are many fair-minded people in this world. In all three cases discussed above--Tim, Paulo, and Jesse--at least one of the people who heard the rumor did not believe the rumormonger.

Conclusion

An adopted child must overcome a great deal, in some cases even a wretched start in life. Yet during his youth there may be an adult who tries to explain away his achievements by spreading unsubstantiated rumors about his age. If an adoptive parent ever comes across this backstabbing, he should remember this. Fair-minded relatives and friends do not believe the rumors. The rumormongering reveals nothing about the child--and a lot about the rumormonger.

FOOD AND THE ADOPTED CHILD[9]

The mysterious acts of adoptees often involve food. Food-related problems can, of course, arise with any youngster. However, there are some additional food-related issues that may need to be considered in the case of an adopted child.[10]

Catch-Up Growth, the Paramount Importance of Food, and Control

Some pediatricians prescribe unlimited food for an adopted child for a full year after his arrival, regardless of the child's native country, age, and weight during that year. Such pediatricians understand the concept of catch-up growth, as illustrated by the story of Jack.[11]

When Jack was adopted at age one from a foreign land, his brunette hair had a reddish tint, his skin had an unhealthy pallor, and his body was very thin except for a distended belly. In other words, the boy exhibited malnutrition. The pediatrician prescribed unlimited food for Jack for one year.

During that year Jack ate large quantities of food. He

---

[9] "Food" was first published in 1995.

[10] According to Dr. Jerri Ann Jenista, there may be medical problems, such as malabsorption, micronutrient deficiencies, parasites, and infections, associated with feeding disorders. Thus, new parents should rule out these problems with a thorough physical examination by a pediatrician before assuming that their child's food issues are primarily behavioral.

[11] The names of minors in this article are fictitious.

often drank five bottles of baby formula a night and ate three large meals and multiple snacks a day. In fact, he ate so much that his parents worried he would make himself sick.

When introduced to new food, Jack always made a face, as if to say, "I'll eat it, but I won't like it." Then, if he really did not like the food, he ate only two servings. Otherwise he had three or more servings. The only new food Jack rejected during the entire year was a dill pickle.

The result was a big increase in height and weight. When Jack arrived in the United States, he ranked only in the 14th percentile in weight and the 25th percentile in height for his age. (In other words, of 100 American boys his age, 86 outweighed him, and 75 were taller.) By the time of the checkup for his second birthday, Jack had jumped to the 70th percentile in weight and the 50th percentile in height. The hearty food consumption had resulted in some catch-ups in weight and height.

Jack's growth that year was not gradual. Rather, it resembled an accordion's movement. He would get plumper and plumper, until well-meaning friends of the family would suggest a diet. Within a week of the advice, Jack would shoot up in height and become almost slender. Then he would repeat the accordion process.

For Jack, like for other malnourished children, food for a time assumed an overriding importance. This paramount importance was expressed in contradictory ways. For example, Jack at times became hysterical if his meal was a few minutes slow to arrive. However, he also threw away food and, like other malnourished children, used it as a means to exercise control in his life.

To signal that he had temporarily finished drinking or eating, Jack would throw the bottle or the remaining food. On stroller rides, he repeatedly tossed his bottle into the dirt. His family solved the beverage-throwing problem by purchasing a bottle strap that attaches to strollers. The boy still hurled the bottle, but it could not hit the ground because of the short strap. However, the food-throwing problem was more complicated.

While most toddlers throw food, few do it like Jack. One or two splat mats are sufficient to contain the mess of most tots. In contrast, Jack, who had a great throwing arm even as a one-year-old, sometimes flung the remnants of his meal all over the kitchen and into two adjoining rooms.

The adoption agency advised Jack's family not to stop him from throwing food until he turned three. According to the agency, the food throwing was an effort by a child to whom food is desperately important to exert some control over his environment.

Jack is now four. He still has a hearty appetite and a willingness to try almost any new food. The boy is sturdy but not overweight. In fact, he eats less as a four-year-old than he did as a one-year-old. His parents are glad they ignored their friends' suggestions and followed the pediatrician's unlimited-food advice.

Happily, Jack no longer throws food. However, with all that practice, his throwing arm is sensational!

Hoarding and Hiding of Food

Some adoptive parents of children with a history of food deprivation find that their child hoards and hides food. This phenomenon is illustrated by the story of Lucy.

The girl arrived in the United States after years of insufficient nourishment. Having known days with nothing to eat, she had learned to plan ahead for those times. Soon after her parents noticed an infestation of ants in her bedroom, they discovered the cause. Lucy had been pocketing extra food from the table to hide under her bed, for the expected future times of want.

Assurances that she would always be well fed in her home clearly left Lucy unconvinced. Then her parents came up with a plan that proved to be a success. They assigned the child a kitchen closet shelf that was hers alone, and they supplied it with edibles such as cereal. For a time, she would check frequently to make sure that her shelf was well stocked. After a while, she did not need to check so often. Eventually, Lucy became satisfied that she would not go hungry.

Food Stealing and Food Punishment

One tot emerged malnourished from a foreign orphanage where big children stole from little ones. The following year, he got into trouble at play school for snatching food from other children's plates during lunches. The teacher was angry because the "greedy" child was "stealing food." A quiet talk between the boy's mother and the teacher resulted in greater understanding on the part of the teacher and extra servings for the child, which soon eliminated the problem.

This boy's parents never deprive him of dinner or a dessert for misbehavior. Someone with a history of hunger needs to be convinced that he will not lack food in his home.

Lactose Intolerance, Bottle Propping, and Delayed Self-Feeding

Not all feeding issues involving adopted children stem from a history of malnutrition or a post-infancy adoption. Three such feeding issues are illustrated by the story of Robin.

When Robin's adoptive parents first met him in Central America, he was a healthy and sturdy three-month-old baby. By asking questions about his baby formula, his new parents discovered that Robin, like a high percentage of Hispanic, Asian, and African children, is lactose-intolerant. The parents were able to solve his problem of intolerance to milk simply by substituting soy formula for a milk-based formula. When Robin is older, he, like many other children, may outgrow this problem and drink milk without adverse effects.

The family also discovered that Robin was accustomed to eating lying down. Although he loved to be held, he clearly did not know how to eat in an upright position, even in his new mother's arms. While being fed, he kept trying to assume a horizontal position. It appears that Robin, like many other babies from orphanages, had been fed lying down, with no one near and the bottle propped in position. This feeding position is potentially dangerous, because it increases the risk of choking. With patience, the boy became accustomed to eating in an upright position.

Robin's parents, who were prevented from adopting him until he was eight months old, discovered the third food issue at the time of the adoption. Many older infants and toddlers, including Robin, arrive from foreign countries with no idea how to feed themselves. The usual explanation is that in cultures in which becoming independent at an early age is disfavored, children are inhibited from feeding themselves until they are older.

The first time eight-month-old Robin was handed a cracker, he seemed surprised at the thought of feeding himself. While he could hold the cracker, he had no idea how to convey it to his mouth. He waited, perplexed, for it to be fed to him. Similarly, when he was bottle-fed in his new mother's arms, he made no effort to hold the bottle and looked surprised when she handed it to him.

After Robin's mother began teaching him to feed himself, things moved quickly. Probably because of being older than many American babies at the start of self-feeding, he learned fast. Once the boy could feed himself, he refused to be fed by anyone else. Always a picky eater, he became even more so after he could control what entered his mouth. At age two Robin, when offered food he did not like, would turn his head away and say, "No way!"

Robin is now four. His food taboos still include meat, poultry, fish, and vegetables. Nonetheless, according to his pediatrician, the boy is doing very well and is healthy, despite his bizarre diet. Following the pediatrician's advice,

Robin's family does not force him to swallow foods he dislikes but does give him a vitamin daily. In short, adopted children, like birth children, can be hearty eaters—or finicky eaters who drive their mothers crazy!

Mixed Reactions to Native Food

Initially, a child adopted internationally may be homesick for his native land and crave his native food. Sympathetic adoptive parents have tried to include this food in some meals. In addition, some parents have treated their child to a meal in a restaurant of his native culture. In some cases the child was delighted. In other cases, including Sam's, the child reacted negatively, to his parents' surprise.

Sam, born in Korea, became agitated when his adoptive parents took him to a Korean restaurant in the United States. In the parents' opinion, he had started identifying with American culture and disengaging from Korean culture. The boy misinterpreted the trip to a restaurant run by Koreans as an effort by his parents to send him back to his old life. He was upset at the prospect of losing his new family and new life. Someday, after Sam has become convinced of the permanency of his family, he should enjoy eating Korean food and meeting Koreans.

Appetite Increase Following Deprivation, Food Gorging, and the Link Between Non-Food Deprivation and Food Problems

Not all speedy weight gains following an adoption placement signal deprivation of food. Many adoptive parents (including Robin's) have found that their new child, though well-nourished, wants to eat much more and more frequently than his previous caretaker had advised. Somehow, being the center of a parent's love and attention quickly results in big appetite increases and surprising weight and height gains for many adoptees.

Some adopted children, including children without a known history of malnutrition, have such huge appetites that they gorge themselves with food to the point of getting stomach aches or vomiting. Courtney is an example.

The girl was adopted from a Russian orphanage when she was about five years old. To her adoptive parents' surprise, she did not know when she was full. Courtney occasionally ate so much that she vomited. A person who did not get enough to eat before the adoption (which is true for many children from orphanages) may not know his stomach limits or believe that food will always be available. Thus, Courtney's gorging may stem from food deprivation. However, some children overeat even though they are not physically hungry.

There is a link in some cases between non-food deprivation before the adoption and gorging or other food problems after the adoption. Food gorging, food hoarding, and food stealing have all been equated to an attempt to fill up the emptiness the child feels inside. (In other words, a youngster starved for affection or with other unmet needs, like an obese adult with unmet needs, may look to food for comfort.) According to some sources, gorging, hoarding, and stealing can be linked to maternal deprivation, inadequate early parenting, or attachment disorders. Maternal deprivation has even been said to be a contributing cause for malnutrition, as well as for failure to thrive.

Breast-Feeding

Yet another food issue concerns nursing. Many adoptive mothers are sad at the thought of their child having missed the breast-feeding experience. It is technically possible for a mother who has not given birth to breast-feed her adopted child, but the successes in this area are rare. For women considering pursuing this option, the La Leche League is a source for information. The league, which is listed in most telephone books, can provide, among other things, a booklet on breast-feeding an adopted baby.

In any event, two things should be kept in mind about nursing. First, some adoptive parents discover that their child did experience breast-feeding before the adoption. Second, not only can food be love, but bottle-feeding a preschooler in the new parent's arms is both food and love. In other words, a child does not need to suck at his mother's breast to feel safe and loved in her arms.

Conclusion

Sometimes food-related issues arise with an adopted child. Most of the issues discussed above are linked to an adoptee's past physical or emotional malnutrition or a hungering for both food and love.

For new parents of children with eating problems, I have a message. Time, love, plenty of good food, and a sense of humor can help you and your child through. For our adopted children I also have a message. Eat, drink (milk or a soy substitute), and be merry!

<u>THE PAST AND THE ADOPTED CHILD</u>[12]

A newly adopted child comes with a past. It is part of him. Therefore, his adoptive parents should learn about the former life.

Unfortunately, many adoptive parents are told little of their child's history. Some of the information they do receive may well be wrong or incomplete. The missing pieces of the puzzle could help the family to solve the child's problems and to appreciate strengths developed by him through adversity. Yet it is not always possible for parents to uncover the facts (<u>e.g.</u>, when adopting an abandoned toddler from abroad).

Even if the past remains a mystery, it colors the present in various ways. They include: (1) regression; (2) readiness; (3) survival behavior; (4) different reactions to similar circumstances; (5) ghosts; (6) flashbacks; and (7) clues to the past. The regression and readiness issues are illustrated by the story of Robin.[13]

<u>Regression and Readiness</u>

Robin was adopted from Central America when he was eight months old. He came from foster care and an orphanage.

At first, the child seemed rather backward. He clung to

---

[12] "Past" was first published in 2012.

[13] All names of minors in this article are aliases to preserve privacy.

his new mother and was interested basically in sleeping, eating, and being held by her. Many older infants crawl around the house to explore their surroundings or to test their independence. Robin's primary use of crawling was to follow his mom from room to room.

By age two, Robin was advanced in some respects. That year he began toilet training. However, he always had an "accident" soon after donning underpants. Robin, who did not respond to praise for being a big boy, turned three still in diapers.

At that point his mother asked him why he was having accidents. He replied, "I like being a baby. And babies wear diapers."

Suddenly, the situation made sense. Robin, with limited experience of infancy in a stable and loving home, just needed more time to be a baby.

The mother decided to wait until he was ready. About two months later, she noticed he had had a growth spurt. When she complimented him on his long "big-boy" legs, Robin seemed pleased. She asked if he wanted to wear big-boy pants that day, and he did. A week later he no longer needed diapers day or night.

The story of Robin illustrates regression and readiness issues that often arise in adoption. Many newly adopted children regress in behavior to a past age. They revert to an earlier developmental stage. Thus, partly due to regression, Robin entered at eight months the mother-child attachment stage, which is more typical of a newborn. For a while, adopted children may also be unready to advance with their peers to the next level on schedule. The usual reason is that the child needs time to adjust from his old life or to engage in catch-up growth (because he is behind physically, mentally, or emotionally). Many youngsters were neglected or abused before their adoption and would benefit from babying--and from postponing kindergarten for a year.

In any event, new adoptive parents should not conclude from a slow start that their child is backward. Robin, who seemed hopeless at toilet training, finished completely with diapers and bed-wetting at a very young age. Like many adopted children, he started a stage late but ended early.

Survival Behavior

A newly adopted child may act strangely. If this mysterious and "bizarre" conduct relates to a hardship in his past, it may be survival behavior. Because malnutrition (physical or emotional) before adoption is so common, the conduct often involves food.

Todd acted strangely. The boy, who had come from an orphanage in India, received ample food from his adoptive family. Yet in school he ate his lunch and then retrieved partially eaten meals from the garbage can for later.

Todd was considered weird by his teacher and classmates. However, his old life had apparently taught him that adults could not be trusted to provide food. It is likely that, having known times of hunger, he was merely taking precautions against being hungry again.

Sara also behaved oddly, leading her adoptive mother to

seek professional advice. The girl refused to fall asleep unless she was clutching a piece of bread.

Sara's apparent problem turned out to be her solution to the real problem. Many malnourished or traumatized orphans slept poorly at first in a new home. The remedy in some cases, including Sara's, was to put the child to bed holding a piece of bread. The youngster could fall asleep knowing he would not go hungry when he awoke.

Different Reactions to Similar Circumstances

Two children may react to the same situation in different ways. Thus, a girl who was sexually molested may pick another abuser for a boyfriend, shun sexual contact, or molest younger children. Sadly, some children respond to sexual or physical abuse by following the abuser's example. They turn into predators themselves.

Similarly, some children who were abandoned by a birth parent desert their own offspring. Others become steadfast parents. In short, a child's past experiences influence his future conduct, but he must decide which path to take.

Ghosts

"Ghosts" from an adopted child's past may haunt the present. Often the ghosts are the birth parents.

Even if the child cannot remember his birth parents, he does think about them. He may idealize or demonize his birth relatives since he knows little about them. This distorted picture affects how he views his adoptive parents and himself.

Other ghosts may appear. For children who experienced

malnutrition, there is the ghost of hunger. People may lie, steal, or cheat if, like Scarlett O'Hara, they are determined never to be hungry again. Thus, Irene, who had been malnourished, stole food from her school mates--but always left their money untouched.

For children who, prior to adoption, suffered from sexual, physical, or emotional abuse, there is the ghost of abuse. Surprisingly, some victims try to get the adoptive parent to abuse them. The child may feel he deserves mistreatment and attempt to goad the new parent into hurting him. Thus, a girl who endured sexual abuse before the adoption may act seductively toward her adoptive father. A boy who experienced verbal or physical abuse may heap abuse on his adoptive mother (e.g., often swearing at her or kicking her).

Adoptive parents try to lay the ghosts to rest. They employ multiple approaches. The best solution depends on the child. The approaches include:

1. The creation of a secure environment in which the parent makes clear, by word and deed, that he loves his child and will take care of him;
2. Psychotherapy;
3. A return to the past (e.g., arranging trips to the child's homeland or contacts between him and his birth family);
4. Talks with the sleeping child; and
5. Prayer.

The first three approaches are self-explanatory. As for the

fourth approach, the newly adopted child needs to learn that he is safe and loved in his new home. One way, in addition to acts, is to tell him when he is awake and when he is asleep. This approach was used with Jack.

Jack was a troubled child who showed symptoms of abuse. Initially, he found it difficult to accept the love of his adoptive parents. He seemed to view the mother, in particular, as an enemy.

The woman tried in various ways to communicate to her son that he was safe and loved. Sometimes she would whisper to him while he slept, and this appeared beneficial. She would say, "It's all right, Jack. You're safe. Your mommy and daddy love you."

The fifth approach calls for a daily prayer. It incorporates a request for help to be a good parent and occasionally includes a progress report to God. The prayer can make a difference even if the person reciting it is not religious. It is a daily reminder that one of his highest priorities in life is to work on being a good parent.

Flashbacks

Flashbacks differ somewhat from ghosts. Flashbacks generally involve an event or object in the present that triggers a striking memory or strong emotion from the past. Troy knows personally about this phenomenon.

Troy was five years old when his Korean birth parents sent him by bus on an errand. He never saw them again because they took off while he was gone. Eventually, the boy became part of an American family. When Troy was a young man, he visited Korea and had flashbacks to the abandonment.

Different events or objects can trigger a flashback. Before being adopted at age one, Jack (discussed above in this article) was taken away from or left by various people. Later that year his adoptive father had to travel overnight on business. Jack experienced a flashback at the sight of the suitcase and of the father waving good-bye.

Jack's parents dealt over time with his fear of abandonment. Most importantly, they gave him a close-knit family. In addition, before every family trip, the mother would line up the luggage of the four members of the household, identify the owner of each suitcase to Jack, and announce, "All four of us are going, and all four of us are coming back." She continued the practice for eight years, until Jack indicated she was stating the obvious.

Clues to the Past

A child's reaction to others or to objects may provide clues to his past. For example, a girl's treatment of her doll (e.g., nurturing or violent) can reveal how she herself was treated.

Clues may point to a past experience that was happy, sad, or shocking. Unfortunately, the child may furnish the clue but be unable to expand on it. For example, Julie occasionally has a mental image. In her mind, the teenager sees her birth father dragging her birth mother by the hair. The scene disturbs the girl, but she cannot explain it. If the mental picture is a memory, there was violence in Julie's birth family, and she was a witness.

Of course, clues can be misleading. They do not guarantee that the incident suspected did occur. Nonetheless, some adoptive parents first became aware from clues that their child suffered sexual or physical abuse prior to the adoption.

If there was abuse, the adoptive parent should take steps to help the child and to break the cycle of violence. Since the child was exposed to bad examples, the parent should begin by setting a good one. Even a baby can learn by example, as shown by the story of Jack (discussed above).

Jack first met his adoptive family when he was about twelve months old. He came from foster care and an orphanage and had repeatedly experienced changes in caretaker.

During the first week, the baby did two things the adoptive parents had never seen their little nephews do. First, every morning he awoke scared and disoriented by his surroundings (and seemed surprised to find his new parents still there). Second, when the parents gave him a teddy bear and a smiling rubber frog, he reacted by hitting and spanking those toys.

Every morning the father would comfort his frightened son. The man would cradle him face to face in his arms. He would gently stroke Jack's head, while looking into his eyes and speaking softly to the child.

For a week Jack continued to be scared and disoriented upon waking and to hit his toys. He seemed to know little about gentle play. Then, early one morning, the mother entered the room to find him awake in the crib. To her surprise, the baby, appearing neither afraid nor bewildered, was comforting his frog. Jack was cradling it face to face in his arms. He was gently stroking the frog's head, while looking into its eyes and babbling softly to the little green toy.

Conclusion

The past leaves wounds. It also helps explain the present. Many adopted children survived traumatic events before their adoption. They bear physical or emotional scars from the past.

Some teenagers find it difficult to admit or forgive what occurred. The past haunts them and blocks them from moving forward. However, if Agathon was right, even God cannot change the past.

So I have a message for our adopted children. You are far more than the sum of your past experiences. With a positive attitude and hard work, you can create a better future. Yesterday is written, but tomorrow belongs to you.

MATCHMAKING AND THE ADOPTED CHILD[14]

There is widespread ignorance about matchmaking for adoption. How is a match made between would-be adoptive parents and a particular child? Some people are sure they know the answer to this mystery. By popular belief, the match occurs because an adoption agency matched the parents' characteristics and preferences with a child. In reality, adoptions, like marriages, come about in various ways. Some of these ways, and the occasionally surprising results, are illustrated by the stories of three mothers.[15]

The Mother of Christine

Dr. Williams, a single woman, applied to an adoption agency. She wanted a little boy or little girl. To adopt a child from Central America through the agency, she had to satisfy the requirements of her state, the United States, and a foreign country. This entailed travel abroad and two home studies, one in each country. The home studies required interviews with social workers and other professionals, criminal checks, psychological tests, character checks, medical tests, and considerable paperwork in English and in Spanish.

After Dr. Williams's name reached the top of the agency's waiting list, she was assigned baby Christine. The

---

[14] "Matchmaking" was first published in 1996.

[15] For privacy reasons, fake names were used in this article.

girl is now four years old. Despite their different coloring, the mother and daughter look strikingly alike. Dr. Williams believes the match was made by God.

Still, the woman was puzzled for a while about the human element involved. She wondered how the social workers had figured out that Christine was destined for her. To find the answer, she contacted her Central American lawyer.

It turns out that, despite two home studies, no social worker or social scientist matched Dr. Williams with her daughter. It was the lawyer (who likes boys to go to couples) who decided to assign the woman an infant girl. However, he was too busy to make the selection personally. Instead, he sent the youngest, lowest-ranking employee in his office off to the orphanage, with instructions to pick out a baby girl for Dr. Williams. In short, this match made in heaven was accomplished through the whim of a teenage girl!

The Mother of Jack

Sometimes would-be parents rule out a physical, mental, or emotional problem in a child and receive a child with that problem anyway. It happened to Jack's mother. This educated, intellectual woman and her husband had to fill out an adoption form listing dozens of physical, mental, and emotional disabilities found in children. They made clear on the form that they would not accept a hyperactive child.

The couple rejected a number of referrals, including an American newborn boy, before learning of Jack. At the time of the referral, he was eleven months old and living in a country to which the would-be parents had not applied. They were able to adopt Jack because the person who would have adopted him had just accepted the newborn boy. In other words, through the adoption agency's intervention, the couple got him by taking somebody else's place on a slow-moving waiting list on which they had never waited.

Jack entered his mother's civilized life like a toddler tornado. For four years he was the most active child wherever he went, and three separate doctors ultimately declared him hyperactive. His play school had more than 100 pupils. According to the staff, Jack was the most all-boy boy in the school, a child with no fear, and the liveliest child in the school.

In adoption, some matches are not made in heaven. However, this match was heaven-sent, as may become clear from seeing Jack's proud and smiling--though occasionally shell-shocked--mother with merry, thriving Jack.

The Mother of Julie and Matt

Some would-be parents specify the sex of the child, the age of the child, or the number of children and get a child of the opposite sex, a child of another age, or a different number of children. All three things happened to Cara.

The woman was sure she knew what she wanted in an adopted child. In fact, she was adamant. According to her, she would adopt only one child, who had to be a baby, a girl, and Korean. Thus, when blond, Caucasian Cara was offered the chance to adopt two blond, Caucasian sisters, she declined.

With pluck and determination, Cara set out to find her child herself. After her husband was transferred by his company to Korea, she went to various Korean agencies and orphanages and met with rejection. She also began talking directly with Koreans considering placing a child for adoption.

Suddenly, after two heartbreaking years of dealing with Korean institutions and birth families, Cara had to prepare for the arrival of "twins." In a three-day period, an adoption agency offered her a two-day-old boy, a birth mother offered her a five-year-old girl, and she accepted both children.

Later she learned why she had been assigned a boy. The match of Cara and her beloved son Matt was accomplished through the prejudice of the Korean social worker. At the time of the assignment, there was a newborn girl available for adoption, and Cara's application had specified a girl. However, the social worker, like many Asians, was prejudiced against girls. The woman simply assumed Cara had made a mistake in filling out the application.

In contrast, the match of Cara and her daughter Julie was, on Cara's side, due to love basically at first sight. The thunderclap sounded during their very first meeting.

This is what happened. Cara while in Korea was introduced by an intermediary to Julie, then five years old, and the girl's birth mother. Later in the meeting the two women were discussing through the interpreter the possible adoption. Cara had had similar conversations in other cases she had decided not to pursue. During this particular discussion, she suddenly realized that Julie was still in the room listening. Cara, with her kind heart, understood how painful such talk must be for a youngster. At her suggestion, the child was sent off to play. On the way out, Julie deliberately slammed the door. At the sound of the crash, strong-willed Cara, recognizing a kindred spirit, fell in love with the little girl.

Matchmaking

Adoptive matchmaking to some extent resembles marital matchmaking. There are multiple parties to satisfy and many ways for the match to occur. For example, in the past:

1. Matchmakers such as social workers proposed a particular child because of a careful matching of the characteristics of the would-be parents and that child, because the parents were next on the waiting list, or because the child was disrupting her orphanage. Matchmakers such as priests, doctors, and friends proposed a match to help a pregnant teenager or an infertile couple. Matchmakers such as foreign lawyers and foreign facilitators proposed a match for money or for humanitarian reasons;

2. Birth parents chose one set of would-be parents over another because the preferred parents were religious, agnostic, or lesbians. In some cases a birth mother selected a particular couple because they would let her visit the child, had a cat, or were the parents she wished she had had;

3. Older children consented to adoption to have a

family or for other reasons of their own; and

4. Would-be parents said yes to a particular child because they fell in love with his smile and bravado on a videotape, she was crying in every single photograph, or this was the first child offered.

In adoptive matchmaking, as in marital matchmaking, many matches are cases of love (e.g., love by the parent of the child's picture) at first sight. Sometimes an abiding love develops slowly.

Often one party to the matchmaking is ready to make a commitment before another party. For example, Cara, discussed above, and Julie's birth mother concluded at the first meeting that Cara and Julie belonged together. However, due to circumstances predating the adoption, it took Julie years after joining her adoptive family to reach the same conclusion.

Sometimes matchmaking that began well ends badly. For example, marital matchmaking can end in a broken engagement before marriage or a divorce after marriage. Similarly, adoptive matchmaking can end in a "disruption" (the name for the situation in which a child placed for adoption is returned before the adoption is finalized) or a "dissolution" (the return of a child after a final adoption).

There are, of course, some differences between matchmaking resulting in adoption and matchmaking resulting in marriage. Perhaps the biggest difference concerns the success rate. Reliable statistics on the percentage of <u>final</u> adoptions that fail are unavailable. This is in part because most published reports focus on disruptions rather than dissolutions, confuse the two categories, combine the two categories, or concentrate on older child adoptions (the most failure-prone). Nonetheless, it is clear that marriages are far more likely to fail than adoptions. Based on U.S. Census Bureau estimates for the early 1990's, approximately 50% of marriages would end in divorce. According to a June 4, 1990, <u>Time</u> article, only "[a]bout 2% of all adoptions in the U.S. fail."

Conclusion

Life can be hard for social workers and other matchmakers. Would-be parents are positive they know what they want in a child but often are mistaken. Sometimes the parents end up with a very different child, and, like the three mothers discussed above, are delighted.

So how the adoptive parents got assigned the child hardly matters. Regardless of the method or the reason for the match, their child may be just what they wanted.

In fact, through adoption, an adoptive parent often gets a beloved child and much more. Adoption frequently leads, for the person adopting, to finding a calling (such as helping orphans abroad); making new friends (<u>e.g.</u>, Asian friends for a parent who adopted from Asia or African-American friends for the white parent of a black child); getting exposed to international travel and a foreign culture; or becoming a citizen of the world. Moreover, the child may possess qualities (e.g., musical, mathematical, or athletic prowess seemingly outside the parent's gene pool) the parent coveted but never had. As one adoptive couple said, "God doesn't always give you what you want. Sometimes God gives you something better."

TOUCHING AND THE ADOPTED CHILD[16]

"Have you hugged your kid today?" asks the bumper sticker. A child needs a hug, a kiss, or other good touching. Would-be adoptive parents generally have pent-up love to give a child. Yet often, after the adoption, the new parents' hugs and kisses are rejected.

Why does the child shun the hugs and kisses? Initially, he may simply dislike personal contact with virtual strangers. However, some children remain uncomfortable with physical displays of affection long after their adoption. In some cases the child is being loyal to a prior caretaker. In other cases the child previously experienced insufficient touching (e.g., in neglect cases), a different type of touching (e.g., several youngsters sharing a bed), or bad touching (e.g., beatings, other physical abuse, or sexual abuse).

All three touching problems can be serious. There are various solutions to these problems, as adoptive parents have discovered, often through trial and error. The three touching problems and some of the attempted solutions are discussed below.

Insufficient Touching

A couple adopted Sam[17] from Korea when he was five years old. Sam's birth mother had both loved him and

---

[16] "Touching" was first published in 1998.

[17] Except for the name of my new niece Alexa, all children's names in this article are pseudonyms.

neglected him, sometimes leaving the child home alone and frightened for hours.

The boy presented a mystery to his adoptive parents from the start. He insisted on wearing his clothing so tight that it left welts on his slender body. Given clothes of the proper size, he would fasten his belt and twist his undergarments so hard that he must have been in pain.

Sam's new mother was determined to find out why her beloved son was hurting himself. It took more than a year and considerable persistence, but she eventually found a professional who succeeded in unraveling the mystery. The too-tight clothing was an attempt by a child desperately in need of hugs to hug himself.

Paradoxically, some children desperate for hugs, including Sam, resist the hugs first offered by their new parents. However, there are alternative forms of good touching for initiating and maintaining physical contact. For example, parents of a little girl can play horsey with her, braid her hair, hold her hand, pat her back, and support her body during a swimming, skating, or gymnastics lesson.

The icebreaker depends on the child's age and past experiences. Some adopted infants and toddlers began to thrive after hours each day of being transported in a Snugli-type baby carrier or held. The icebreaker for some older children was gentle tickling or good-natured roughhousing. The icebreaker between one girl and her new mother was reading together daily in a rocking chair. Because the focus was on the story rather than the touching, the girl could accept the physical contact.

Many previously neglected children welcome hugs and other physical contact from their new parents within days. However, some children quickly become attached to one parent (usually the mother) but avoid the other. For example, a baby boy from a Central American orphanage promptly bonded with the mother but for nearly three years basically avoided the father. Whenever the man tried the exuberant roughhousing the boy's older sibling had loved at the same age, the child wailed. The icebreaker turned out to be repeated father-son sessions of slow-motion roughhousing.

Touch deprivation and other touching problems can lead to attachment disorders. In some cases where a child seemed incapable of attaching to anybody, it was deemed advisable for one parent to handle the feeding and touching until the youngster bonded with that parent. Subsequently, the other parent participated and became a beneficiary of the child's newfound ability to attach.

Frequent good touching (plus good parenting) by a caring adoptive parent may prevent or solve attachment disorders. A 1996 Jewel Among Jewels Adoption News article quoted Dr. Gregory Keck, an attachment specialist, on attachment disorders and the newly adopted infant who dislikes being touched. Dr. Keck said, "If adoptive parents . . . would hold the child closely, forcing him to be cuddled, and just didn't put him down for the next month, you probably would have a whole different outcome."

A similar strategy may benefit an older child who

dislikes being touched. A social worker knowledgeable about attachment disorders adopted a seven-year-old girl from a Russian orphanage. This new mother refused to accept a "standoffish" daughter and "kept being in her face" with good touching. Within a year the daughter between activities was voluntarily seeking out the mother for a quick hug.

Unfortunately, diagnosing touch deprivation can be tricky. The symptoms vary, and the child often cannot verbalize the underlying problem. As discussed above, Sam attempted to hug himself through constrictive clothing. A girl in a busy birth family tried to hug herself nightly in bed by squeezing herself into the crack between the mattress and the wall. (She is now an adult alcoholic.) A girl in an unloving birth family sought the holding she craved through sexual promiscuity. Some adopted youngsters exhibited physical, emotional, and learning problems requiring treatment, mostly because these children had spent their infancy in orphanages providing little human contact. Some infants deprived of adequate good touching turned into failure-to-thrive babies; they stopped growing or even stopped eating.

Touch deprivation, when coupled with other emotional deprivation, can be fatal. For lack of touching and emotional nurture, some children in institutions died before finding a good home.

Different Touching

Sometimes a child's need for human touch was met before the adoption by a different touching from that offered by his new parent. For example, numerous children have arrived from Korea unaccustomed to hugging, kissing, or a man's affectionate touch. However, during their early childhood in Korea, many of them were carried around strapped to a woman's back or slept nightly with a female relative. To children adopted from a culture or family where parental hugs and kisses are absent, hugs and kisses can seem alien--or taboo. Such children have been known to respond to hugs by stiffening, crying, or striking the new parent.

Because the two cultures or two families express affection differently, miscommunication can result. The new parent may equate kisses with love, but the child may not and may miss a different touching. Despite kisses, he can for a time feel unloved in his new family. To compound the problem, the new parent may not know about, be willing to supply, or be able to provide the child's preferred touching (e.g., the whole family sleeping in one bed).

The preferred touching varies depending on the adopted child's age, birth country, and personal circumstances. However, for foreign-born infants and toddlers like Jack, the preferred touching may be breast-feeding.

Jack was adopted at age one from a foreign orphanage. The orphanage, which had only female caretakers, had a mortality rate allegedly over 50%. Prior to entering the orphanage, he had lived with his birth mother. She, like most mothers in that country, breast-fed a baby.

Like many adopted children, Jack exhibited all three touching problems. Based on what his adoptive parents could uncover, he had received insufficient good touching, had been weaned suddenly from breast-feeding, and had been hit.

Jack's adoptive mother could not breast-feed him, to duplicate the earlier touching. The child sought comfort in a baby bottle, from which he refused to be weaned. When he was two years old, a pediatrician said Jack would soon give up the bottle because of teasing from friends. The boy got teased by friends and strangers; he ignored the teasing. He turned five before he completely gave up his bottle.

To complicate Jack's touching problems, he at that stage preferred, after his experience with the orphanage women, the company of men and had Attention Deficit/Hyperactivity Disorder. The child could not stay still. The first year after the adoption, his mother generally had to chase him to hug him, and he would soon struggle to keep moving. As for lap-sitting, within ten seconds his attention would wander, and he would flail around to escape. As for being kissed, he not infrequently would rub off the kiss.

One day, after Jack wiped off his mother's kiss, she started the "Kiss-Off Game." This game converts what otherwise might be rejection of the parent by the child into their shared rejection of a kiss. If Jack rejected her kiss, she would rub it off, try another kiss, rub that one off if it got rejected, and then try again. ("Was this kiss better?" "No." "Then take it away. Was this one better?" "No." "You mean you didn't like my 'wonderful' kiss?!") The Kiss-Off Game included "good" kisses such as a light smooch on the hair and wonderfully "bad" (i.e., silly) kisses, including a snuffling doggy kiss and a loud "razzberry" kiss. At first the boy rejected all the kisses, so his mother vigorously rubbed them all off. However, after playing the game a few times, he began to admit to liking one or two kisses. Jack finally was getting multiple kisses and keeping some, in a joking atmosphere.

Subsequently, a new game evolved. This "Good Kiss/ Bad Kiss Game" gave the boy a choice between a good kiss and a bad kiss. If Jack wiped away or refused his mother's good-bye kiss before leaving the house for school, she would react with mock horror and "threaten" him with a bad kiss. She might say, "Oh, poor child, you're going to get such a slimy, yucky kiss later. It's your choice--good kiss now or bad kiss later." Generally Jack, laughing, would run to her for his good kiss. If not, she would pounce on him later, give him a bad kiss, and accept with feigned dismay a bad kiss in return.

Jack's mother also hugged him as best she could. In addition, she sought help from his play-school teachers. She told them she did not care whether he learned the alphabet and numbers; what he needed from them was hugs.[18]

Things changed over time for the boy who fled from

---

[18] A contrary view calls for the mother and father of a child resistant to hugs to restrict for a time the group giving the hugs to the parents. This approach has the benefit of reinforcing in the child's mind the position of his parents as his main source of love and comfort.

hugs and rubbed off kisses. At six years old, Jack some nights would race his younger sibling to sit in their mother's lap. Sometimes both youngsters would nestle together in her lap. On school days Jack, at his initiative, and his parent would kiss good-bye at the bus stop, while other children (who considered kissing a relative in public uncool) watched. That year Jack was the only child getting kissed at the bus stop, but he wanted his kiss anyway.

Bad Touching

Sexual abuse and physical abuse are the two worst forms of bad touching. Sadly, many adopted children were victims of abuse prior to adoption. In some cases the child was removed from his birth family for that reason; in other cases he suffered abuse while in foster care or an institution. Estimates of the extent of the problem vary. However, based on information in 1995 and 1996 Adoptive Families articles, at least 75% of the children in foster care in the United States were victims of sexual abuse, physical abuse, or both.

Sexual abuse and physical abuse can devastate a child. The child's devastation may reveal itself in different ways, from near-catatonia to violence. Two stories told to me, about the "Puddle Girl" and the "Wild Beast Girl," illustrate the two extremes.

The Puddle Girl lived in the same orphanage as Jack. At the time she was four years old and terrified of men due to sexual abuse by her father.

A mailman and his psychologist wife learned of the Puddle Girl. The couple had sons and wanted a daughter.

The psychologist agreed with her foreign counterpart that the couple would fly to the girl's country and, if things worked out, pursue the adoption.

The mailman tried to initiate interaction with the troubled youngster at their meetings. Her invariable response was to collapse on the floor and just lie there the whole time like a puddle.

Both might-have-been adoptive parents cried as they told me the story. They did not adopt the Puddle Girl. After the trauma of the bad touching, the child preferred her hellhole of an orphanage to a home with a man in it.

Similarly, the Wild Beast Girl was sexually abused at a young age by her father. Subsequently, she was placed in a Korean orphanage. There she attacked anyone who came near her and terrorized the orphanage. Nobody could get close enough to her to comb her hair. With her unkempt hair, homely face, and ferocity, she looked like a wild beast.

One day a minister and his wife arrived at the orphanage. They were adopting a baby boy. The orphanage asked the couple also to take the girl who had turned violent from bad touching. The couple refused. After some begging, the two left and prayed over the decision. Subsequently, they said no again. Following more begging, they again departed and prayed. Afterwards, they agreed to adopt both children.

Where Are They Now?

The five-year-old boy who tried to hug himself through too-tight clothing is now nine. After his arrival in America, Sam had trouble coping with hugs and other physical displays of affection. For a time, like many newly adopted children, he also regressed and acted almost infantile. His adoptive mother hurt her back carrying him around. Despite the injury, she continued to carry him sometimes; he seemed to need babying so badly. During the day Sam was a very needy child. During the night he popped out of bed repeatedly to check whether his parents were still there. Eventually, the parents persuaded him that they, unlike his birth mother, would not slip away and leave him home alone. Sam now likes baggy clothes. A delightful boy, he is affectionate and increasingly like his warm-hearted mother. The two are very close. Yet the past leaves wounds. The mother, making a point that also applies to other children discussed above, said, "Sam will always have a small hole in his heart."

The hyperactive toddler who was weaned abruptly is now seven. Jack is a very oral child, a very demanding child, and a very lovable child. During the past year, in a natural development, he has begun to reduce his lap-sitting and kisses. At home he still sits on his mother's lap about four times a week. He may be overflowing her lap, he may be bouncing around, but he is by choice there. At school the boy is popular and is in the advanced reading program. Recently, I saw him at the bus stop. When the school bus arrived, Jack raced over to his mother and kissed her good-bye. Then the other students followed his example and kissed their mothers!

The Puddle Girl is now ten--if she survived her deadly

orphanage. Sometimes an all-female adoptive family is found for a girl who was sexually molested. I do not know what happened to this poor child.

The Wild Beast Girl is now an adult. Initially, the girl rejected her new family. For a time her new father daily held her forcibly while he read. To try to escape, she bit him repeatedly. This man of God responded to each bite with a gentle pat. Apparently, it took her parents a lot of work and good touching. Ultimately, she turned into a lovely young lady of whom they can be very proud.

Conclusion

In an imperfect world, adoption often joins together a woman whose arms ache for a child to hug with a child yearning for hugs. It unites a man eager to have a child ride on his shoulders with a child who missed out on riding high.

So welcome home, Alexa and other children about to be adopted from orphanages around the world. Your new parents are ready to hug you!

LANGUAGE AND THE ADOPTED CHILD[19]

Most children are born capable of learning to speak any language. The experience of many young immigrants, including children adopted internationally, supports this view.

Basically, the language development process is supposed to work as follows. The newborn begins the process by crying. He may cry because he is hurt, scared, or hungry, and his parent responds to his distress. The infant soon learns that crying gets results. Day after day, the parent talks to the baby while caring for him. The infant tries out more sounds, and the parent responds positively. Eventually, the baby begins to imitate the words he hears. By twelve months of age, he babbles something recognizable to his parent as a word and is rewarded by the parent's delight. In language development, comprehension generally precedes speech. At fifteen months, the child understands some sentences but may use only five words. By twenty-four months, he says a three-word sentence. The process includes trial and error. For example, a youngster will elicit more comprehension from an English-speaking parent from one word in English (e.g., "juice") than from a complete sentence babbled by chance in Chinese. Since the use of English is rewarded (e.g., getting the juice), this child ends up speaking English.

Unfortunately, for some adopted children, the language

---

[19] "Language" was first published in 1999.

development process went awry. For example, an infant may come from an orphanage where nobody responded to his cries. Because making sounds got no results, the baby may essentially have stopped vocalizing. A foreign-born toddler may have cracked the code to understanding some of his native language and have begun to talk that language. Then he flies to the United States to people speaking English and must start over. The tot may respond with rage to his sudden inability to understand and to communicate. An older child maybe was neglected or had caretakers who rarely talked to him. With few words to mimic and little reinforcement of his verbal efforts, the youngster may be backward in language development. The stories of Melissa, Jack, and Robin[20] illustrate language problems faced by some adopted children.

Melissa

Melissa was five months old when she left her foster family in Korea to join her adoptive family in the United States. Her new family included a father, a mother, and their biological son. She arrived already babbling.

At first, the baby's babble sounded discordant and "foreign" to her American mother. Apparently, Melissa before her arrival had started to imitate the Korean sound combinations uttered around her and was on the path to speaking Korean. She continued the foreign-sounding prattle for a time. Then for a period she babbled in a monotone.

---

[20] The names in this article are fake to protect the children's privacy.

Subsequently, her babble sounded normal to the mother.

Melissa ended up speaking English rather than Korean. Currently she is in high school, where she earns good grades.

Jack

Jack was farther than Melissa on the path to learning the native language when he switched languages. He flew at fifteen months of age to the United States from Latin America, where he had experienced at least six changes of home and of primary caretaker. At the time of the flight, Jack was on the brink of speaking Spanish. Though he arrived speaking no Spanish or English, he said his first English word in September, the month of his arrival.

Jack's desire to be heard was boundless, even if his vocabulary was limited. Starting in infancy, this toddler understood that sound meant communication and noise got results. He roused his adoptive parents at night by loud crying or lusty yells. When he was dissatisfied, everyone within earshot knew it!

That November Jack attended a Thanksgiving dinner. His cousin, who was months older and could talk more, was among the guests. The two boys sat in high chairs opposite each other at the meal. Jack began the discussion with his cousin with a string of nonsense syllables across the table. The cousin responded with a few words from his small vocabulary. This was met by more jabbering from Jack. Soon the toddlers were yelling happy gibberish at each other in turn across the table. It was merry bedlam for most of the feast.

In December Jack's parents threw a large party. Jack apparently noticed that his parents were talking to first one guest and then another. Although many guests were strangers to him, he also circulated among them, engaging one stranger after another in an animated conversation. His side of the conversation was gibberish.

The child was baptized later that month. At the ceremony Jack babbled at high speed, drowned out the priest, and tried to dive headfirst from his mother's arms into the baptismal font.

In February at twenty months old, the boy looked at something and said his first sentence ("What is it?"). Ever curious, he wanted to know the name of everything.

Before and after his first sentence, Jack often talked or sang to himself in his crib in nonsense syllables. He loved putting together different sound combinations in a song. At that stage he also answered "no" to virtually every question and direction. Like most toddlers, he loved saying no.

One evening in April, his mother found him singing a real word over and over on different notes, as if practicing scales. To her mirth, this was not a word he needed to practice. Jack was singing, "No! No! No!"

Over time the boy caught up with his friends in language and surpassed many of them. He said his first seven-word sentence before he was two and a half. According to a pediatrician, Jack at three had a large vocabulary for his age.

In first grade the boy started weekly Spanish lessons. His Spanish pronunciation is very good. This is conceivably due as much to his prior constant practice of multiple sound combinations as to living for his first fifteen months in a Spanish-speaking environment.

Recently, Jack finished first grade. This very verbal, intelligent child had triumphed over his early language difficulties. On the last day of school, he received a perfect report card and the certificate for the best student in the class.

Robin

In terms of readiness to vocalize, Robin was the opposite of Jack. Robin was adopted as an infant from Central America. Prior to the adoption, he had been in an orphanage and in foster care.

From the start there were signs that the baby had been neglected. For example, he could not go to sleep without head banging, and he kept trying to eat even solid food lying down. Head banging and a horizontal eating pattern can mean that an infant remained in a crib for most of the day and fed himself lying down from a bottle "propped" in position (i.e., he was largely unattended, even at mealtime). To add to the parents' surprise, Robin seemed not to know how to cry.

Possible explanations for a baby's not crying include: (1) he is deaf; (2) hyper-attentive caretakers had satisfied his needs before his having to cry to express them; and (3) he was neglected. For Robin, it was easy to rule out the first two possibilities.

Robin proved to be a cheery, gentle, and silent baby. At

nine months old, he did not babble. When he was in distress, he might give a faint whimper.

Robin's pediatrician found the infant to be backward in language. When the boy was eleven months old, he said his first word, "Daddy." Subsequently, he reverted to being essentially soundless.

Still, given adequate provocation, Robin could talk. On one car trip his older sibling prefaced nearly every sentence with, "You know what? You know what?" A parent would respond with "What?" After about 100 miles of you-know-whats, silent Robin, trapped in his baby seat, could stand it no longer. When his sibling once again posed the double question, Robin replied, "What?!"

Between twelve and eighteen months of age, Robin said a number of words. Generally he uttered a word once and then did not use it again. Yet he did show surprising intelligence on several occasions. One concerned a play-school refrigerator.

On school days the toddlers in Robin's class lounged with their bottles on bean-bag chairs. However, they could do this only at specified times. In part because children had been grabbing any bottle from the refrigerator, the school had added a so-called "lock." This fastener kept the tots out of the refrigerator. One day when Robin was at most seventeen months old, he decided it was bottle time.

What followed amazed the teachers. The boy went to the refrigerator, worked open the fastener, and opened the door. He picked out from more than ten baby bottles his bottle and the bottle of his girlfriend. Robin walked over to the girl, handed over her bottle, and pushed her gently onto a bean bag. Then he reclined on another bean bag, and they drank their bottles together.

When Robin was eighteen months old, his mother took him to the pediatrician for a checkup. The tot was doing well in everything but language. At the checkup, the mother expressed concern about his practice of saying a word only once. Then she gave as an example that months earlier he had said "teeth" and had never since used that word. There was a pause. Then behind her a small voice said nonchalantly, "Teeth." It was Robin.

After hearing the toddler's retort and the refrigerator story, the pediatrician thought that Robin was very smart. In her view, he employed a word once and then felt no need to use it again. Another possible reason for his virtual silence was that he was a second child (with an older sibling with logorrhea). The doctor told the mother to reinforce every effort on Robin's part to talk. The following month he said his first sentence ("That's a truck").

For several years Robin's mother parroted everything she understood him to say, to confirm it was comprehensible and to help with pronunciation. However, his speech was so slurred that often even his mother could not understand him. He lagged behind all his play-school classmates in his ability to make himself understood. Typically, only a few family members and teachers understood him when he talked. Robin continued his custom of not practicing sound combinations. However, because he said things on more than one occasion, some of his statements eventually became clear.

For example, from a young age Robin, offered food he did not like, would turn his head away and say something. For months his mother knew only that the statement was negative and ended in an exclamation point. One day when he was two years old, he spoke more clearly than usual. The mother finally understood him and laughed. Faced with food he did not like, Robin said, "No way!"

For much of his early childhood, Robin seemed to his mother to be a mute, amused observer of family life. Once when she was chasing her mischievous older child, she spotted Robin watching them from his high chair with the familiar look of amusement on his face. She asked Robin if he found them funny. He grinned and nodded.

Pronounced delays in speech can indicate retardation. Fortunately, Robin occasionally showed that he was paying attention and absorbing things.

For example, while Robin was in diapers, he sometimes broke his silence through participation in family car games. He did this the first time for the "Locomotion Game." In this game the first player to spot and call out the name of a vehicle (a boat, fire truck, police car, ambulance, motorcycle, airplane, or helicopter) scores another point. One day Robin's relatives were playing the game while traveling in the countryside. Suddenly, Robin from his baby seat called out, "Boat." His family was pleased, but puzzled by his claim to see a boat in the middle of nowhere. The riddle was solved moments later when a truck towing a boat passed the car.

Robin was two and still in diapers when he revealed his understanding of a harder car game. In this game the players take turns naming a different thing in the specified category (e.g., sticky, heavy, or green), with each player dropping out when he runs out of ideas for the category. One day when Robin's relatives were naming things that are sharp, he suddenly joined in with a correct response. The mother was stunned, because Robin so rarely spoke and was still a toddler. However, that night she recalled that his answer had been used in a things-that-are-sharp game on earlier occasions (meaning his answer might reflect a good memory or lucky guess rather than comprehension of the category and game). The following day she decided to test whether Robin really could figure out something in a category. She explained to him that they were playing things that are wet. Then she asked him to name something wet. Robin's response had never before been used in a game. He answered promptly and, it turned out, truthfully, "Diaper."

For a considerable period Robin's communication basically remained non-verbal. For example, for several more years, when he needed something during the night, he did not call his mother. Instead, he would walk to her bedroom and touch her gently. She would awake and find the child standing silently by her bed.

When Robin was three, it became clear that during his

silent period he had been a sponge and had developed a good memory. He could say numerous words, to the extent that his surprised grandmother described his vocabulary as "vast." The boy continued to observe people. Once when the grandmother repeated something she had said on several prior visits, Robin, who was playing quietly nearby, remarked, "I knew you'd mention that."

At three, Robin cried easily. Some parents would have told him not to be a crybaby. However, his mother felt that, by crying, he was communicating and was making up for the unshed tears.

When Robin was four, his mother noticed that he was still behind his play-school classmates in speech, though not in vocabulary. She took him for a professional evaluation. The boy was tested in six areas, including speech, hearing skills, and fine motor skills. He passed all six areas and was said to be advanced in every area but speech. That year he read his first book.

Recently, Robin turned five, too late to qualify for kindergarten. He speaks freely but less distinctly than many children his age and mispronounces some words (e.g., "then" as "den," "thing" as "sing," and "look" as "wook"). While Robin may need a little speech therapy in the next few years, it is clear this bright child is behind in little else. He has overcome the neglect that kept him silent. At a parent-teacher conference this month to discuss readiness for kindergarten, the teacher announced that Robin can skip kindergarten and begin with first grade.

Conclusion

As Ecclesiastes said, for everything there is a season: a time to be born, and a time to die; a time to be silent, and a time to speak. So, new adoptive parents, the time for your child to speak, speak in sentences, or speak your language may arrive late--but be all the more precious for the wait.

Adopted children, you may be slower than your friends to learn a language, because of your switching countries or other personal difficulties. However, your season to speak is here. We parents are eager to hear you talk. We are ready to listen to your words--even to, "No! No! No!"

SIBLINGS AND THE ADOPTED CHILD[21]

The arrival of a new sibling can rock a child's world. He may start to feel like a first wife whose husband brings home a second. Adding a new family member can be tough on someone born in the family--and tougher on an adopted child. Biological children, unlike adoptees, know the security of being in the family from birth. In any event, no new sibling can fulfill an incumbent child's fantasy of the perfect brother or sister.

To compound the problem, the newcomer, if adopted, may mystify (or dumbfound) others by acting "weird." For example, a plump American girl hunted, after preschool meals, for crumbs under the table and food in the garbage can. Allegedly, every child adopted after infancy does at least one thing that seems bizarre to his new family. The weird acts often involve what two experts on adopted children, Dr. Margaret Hostetter and Dr. Dana Johnson,[22] called "survival" behavior. (The preschooler who ate crumbs and garbage had, prior to adoption, been neglected and hospitalized for malnutrition.)

A child may engage in survival behavior in response to neglect, abuse, or other traumatic conditions. The behavior, explainable under the original circumstances, may persist for

---

[21] "Siblings" was first published in 1999.

[22] All names were changed for this article, except for those of Margaret Hostetter, Dana Johnson, Edith Coe, and Philip.

a time after circumstances change. For example, one girl, sexually abused before adoption, slept after adoption on the floor with her back to the wall, armed with whatever weapon she could find. The behavior may shock the adoptive family. (How many children who sleep with a teddy bear expect a new sister who sleeps with a weapon?) Perhaps because many adoptees experienced physical or emotional malnutrition prior to the adoption, survival behavior frequently involves food.

The adopted newcomer may present additional challenges. He may be of a different race, culture, or social class from an incumbent child. If the newcomer experienced hard times before the adoption, he may be needy, violent, vulnerable, or unaccustomed to family life. His troubles may temporarily overwhelm the parents, leaving them little time for the other children. Yet a hard-knocks child often brings joy to the family. The stories of Philip, Susie, Courtney, Sam, and Katya address the arrival of a new sibling by adoption.

Philip

Although the adoption of a child can temporarily rock the world of another child in the family, it can also make that world a gentler place. For most people, the longest relationship of their life is with a brother or sister. Many siblings, including siblings by adoption, help and love each other long after the death of their parents.

"A Letter to Philip" provides an example of more than seven decades of sibling devotion involving an adopted child. Edith Coe wrote the letter, which was published in the spring 1998 issue of <u>Jewel Among Jewels Adoption News</u>. When she and her big brother were children, their parents adopted a sickly infant. They called him Philip. Decades passed, the children grew up, and some family members died. Finally, Edith, the oldest surviving member of the family, was in her late seventies.

At that time she wrote a letter to her little brother. It expressed her feelings for him over their long life together. The letter said, "Philip, have you any idea how much I love and appreciate you? From the frail, five-month-old baby to the seventy-two-year-old man you are today, you have been my very special brother. . . . Philip, what a wonder you were and have been for 72 years!"

Susie

Sometimes it seems that a child in the family and a newly adopted child will never care for each other. This was true for George and Susie.

Initially, George was an only child. His father, a graduate of the Massachusetts Institute of Technology, wanted his offspring to be good in science and to follow in his footsteps. Unfortunately, the boy was not science-minded.

Then George's parents adopted Susie. She came from Vietnam, where she had known hard times. Whatever George was expecting for a sister, it was not Susie.

The little girl soon shocked her new family with her eating behavior. When the mother brought food to the table, Susie darted over, snatched food from a plate, and ran to a corner. There she devoured the food, with her back to the wall and one hand guarding her mouth.

To a middle-class American boy, this behavior must have seemed weird. However, it can be survival behavior for a child who formerly had to live on the street or to defend against bigger children prepared to grab food right out of her mouth.

For years George and Susie got along poorly. It did not help that the girl excelled in math and science. Eventually, both children grew up and left home, Susie after being accepted by an institute of technology.

The two were expected to go their separate ways. Instead, they maintained contact and continued to meet. When their mother expressed surprise, they were surprised. George and Susie said they really like each other!

Courtney

All children are different. Yet the differences between a newly adopted child and another child in the family may surprise the adoptive parents. This happened with Courtney.

The girl was adopted from a Russian orphanage when she was about five years old. Her new family included a couple and their biological son, Tyler. The adoptive parents were happy to have a daughter. However, the adoptive mother had apparently expected her to be the female version of Tyler.

The mother sometimes compared Courtney unfavorably to Tyler. In conversations with friends, the woman would mention, in a disapproving tone, something the girl had done and observe that Tyler had not done that at the same age. Her principal complaint concerned Courtney's "weird" behavior. To the parents' surprise, the daughter did not know when she was full. She occasionally ate so much that she vomited. As the mother pointed out, Tyler did not do that at Courtney's age.

In fact, this food gorging can be survival behavior. Gorging sometimes stems from food or non-food deprivation. If a person did not get enough to eat before the adoption (which is true for many children from orphanages), he may not know his food limits or believe that food will always be available. Similarly, if a person suffered maternal deprivation, he may later attempt through gorging to fill the emptiness he feels inside. In other words, physical or emotional malnutrition leads some children to gorge when food is plentiful.

Tyler and Courtney were indeed different. The key difference was not what they did at age five, but what they had experienced by then. At five, Tyler, a child of privilege, had enjoyed five years of security in his loving family, free from hunger and want. Never having gone hungry, he had learned his food limits and expected food to arrive as needed. At five, Courtney, an orphanage child, was just starting over after losing virtually everything. Her losses included her original home, her homeland, her culture, her language, both her birth parents, any birth siblings, all of her other blood relatives, and all of her friends. In short, the little girl had survived a five-year period that would have devastated many adults.

Sam and Katya

Sometimes the adoption of a child can jeopardize the adjustment of an adoptee already in the family. This happened to Sam.

Sam is a child who needs to know the whereabouts of his parents and who has problems with good-byes. There are reasons for his insecurity. The boy was born in Korea. When he was small, his birth mother repeatedly slipped out with no warning and left him home alone for hours. Then, when he was five, she explained that she had arranged for him to visit his birth father in the United States. In reality, she had arranged for her son to be adopted by a childless American couple. Sam said good-bye to his birth mother believing that he would soon return home. Thus, at an early age he had learned that a parent could suddenly disappear without warning, that a parent could not be trusted, and that a parent's "au revoir" could mean "good-bye."

When Sam arrived in America, his adoptive parents had to deal with the lies. Eventually, he began to believe that his parents would not walk out on him.

After Sam had been in his American home for about four years, the parents decided to adopt again. The couple, who no longer qualified for a Korean adoption, applied to Russia for a daughter.

Sam's mother was to travel alone to Russia. Before saying good-bye, she promised him she would return. Unfortunately, complications in Russia extended the trip. For more than a month the child was without his mom. He spoke occasionally with her by telephone. As time passed, Sam began to deny that it was her voice on the phone, and he announced that his mother had died. Despite the phone conversations, he persisted in calling her dead.

Finally, the mother came home, accompanied by four-year-old Katya. Sam was handsome, black-haired, and tall. Katya was pretty, blonde, and tiny.

From the start, Sam wanted to get rid of his little sister, and Katya was crazy about her big brother. To his anger, she tagged along after him. He beheaded her beloved Barbie doll. She cried but continued to follow him around. Over and over he said the same mean things to her. Grateful for any attention from him and not understanding his English, she would respond adoringly, "Sam! Sam!"

The boy would say to his sister, "I hate you, Katya. Dad hates you. Mom hates you. Everybody here hates you, Katya. Go back to Russia."

Katya would reply adoringly, "Sam! Sam!"

The trip to Russia damaged the relationship between Sam and his family. The boy rejected his parents, apparently no longer believing in their love for him. Though he was in emotional pain, he refused to let himself be loved by anyone. Sam's mother was heart-stricken. She feared that by adopting a second child she had lost her first.

After a wretched period of about nine months, the situation improved greatly. Sam accepted his sister and the continuation of his parents' love. Except for normal sibling disagreements, he is now a caring and protective brother to

Katya. However, one thing did not change. Little Katya still adores big Sam.

Conclusion

There are major disadvantages in life, especially for an adoptee, to being an only child. Sometimes problems arise when the parents of one child adopt another. Nonetheless, one of the best gifts adoptive parents can give their child is a brother or sister.

Indeed, a sibling may be a necessity for an adopted child. Many adopted youngsters were or felt abandoned by a birth parent. Some were actual or virtual orphans before the adoption. They know what it is to feel unwanted, to come from an orphanage, or to be alone in the world. Not surprisingly, many adoptees, like big Sam, fear a second abandonment (including via death or divorce) by a parent. Yet, in this era of increasing life expectancies, babies who are adopted by thirty-year-old parents may well outlive their parents by fifty years (or more). A half-century is a long time to be an orphan with no siblings.

THE "PRIMAL WOUND"
AND THE ADOPTED CHILD[23]

Why do too many children adopted in infancy get into serious trouble (e.g., attempted suicide, sexual promiscuity, drug abuse, or criminal arrests) as teenagers? Nancy Verrier presented a possible answer to this mystery. According to her books, a primal wound develops when a baby and his mother are separated by adoption shortly after childbirth. Severing their connection, which began in the uterus, causes the wound. Allegedly, the wound often manifests itself in adoptees in depression, anxiety, mistrust, abandonment and loss issues, behavioral problems, emotional problems, and difficulties in relationships with significant others.

Proponents of this theory view the separation from the birth mother as the fundamental cause of the depression, anxiety, etc. For example, in writings concerning the separation, Ms. Verrier uses the terminology "the one 'fatal' decision," "life-threatening event," "dynamics that were set in motion at relinquishment," "result of prolonged separation from the mother," "[a]ll of these symptoms . . . can be traced back to the primal wound," "[t]he wound affects adoptees all their lives," "life-long consequences," "the ultimate loss," and "the most devastating loss in the world."

By making the separation primal, the theory minimizes prenatal problems. It also minimizes postnatal traumas that

---

[23] "Primal Wound" was first published in 2015.

sometimes trigger the separation (e.g., the infant was abused, neglected, or addicted to heroin). (In Ms. Verrier's view, the "experience of relinquishment has been the most difficult thing a baby can endure.") This article will focus on some of the prenatal problems.

Except for the forming of the child-mother bond, the primal wound theory gives little weight to the intrauterine life of the adopted baby. Was the newborn, despite months in the womb, basically a blank slate - and therefore fine - until getting badly scarred by the parting from his mother?

I am qualified to address this question (and its answer is no). First, as an attorney, I often dealt with causation (the "but for" event). Second, I am a volunteer in the neonatal and pediatric wards of a major hospital. Since the late 1980's I have spent time one-on-one with hundreds of babies and toddlers, including many premature infants who should still have been in utero. Third, I learned and wrote a lot about adoptees over the years. I am an adoptive mother and adoptive aunt, including to young adults from Asia, Latin America, and Russia, and my adoption-related articles have been published more than 50 times.

Prior generations believed that a pregnant woman should lead a peaceful life for the good of her unborn child. However, extramarital pregnancies are often highly stressful, as illustrated by the one case in which I became involved.

It concerned Thao,[24] a lovely young woman from an

---

[24] This is a fictitious name.

immigrant Asian family. Her boyfriend, whom she loved, moved to California. Thao declined to accompany him because he was not offering marriage. Soon after, she met a man of a different race at a party. He turned out to be a drug dealer and an ex-convict who had spent time in prison for malicious wounding. After getting pregnant, Thao repeatedly asked him for money for an abortion. He deliberately strung her along until too late. For months she successfully hid her pregnancy from her parents, though she lived with them. In her culture, a daughter in her situation brings shame on the entire family. When she was eight months pregnant, her mother guessed. In the ensuing uproar, Thao fled her home. She and the drug dealer, from whom she had separated, made different plans. She wanted an adoption agency to find new parents for her child-to-be, so I introduced her to an agency. He wanted his fourteen-year-old sister, who hated school, to drop out to rear his daughter in an apartment at his expense. Any subsequent problems of this baby cannot be attributed to the removal from the birth mother because there was no adoption. To stop the father from getting the girl, the mother kept her. The last I heard, both the woman and the infant had moved in with the California boyfriend, who was still not offering marriage.

According to the primal wound theory, a fetus bonds with its mother. Generally the woman also bonds with her fetus. Yet in most cases involving young, unmarried females, such as the case above, the pregnancy was traumatic. Often that period includes: (1) the mother's denial to herself that she is pregnant; (2) then fear or dismay; (3) then her attempts to terminate the pregnancy (exercising feverishly, falling on her stomach, ingesting something meant to end the pregnancy, saving money for an abortion, or taking other steps toward killing the baby); (4) trying to conceal from family members and others the existence of her unborn child; (5) enduring the anger and disappointment of relatives after her pregnancy is revealed; (6) facing ridicule or scorn as news of her pregnancy spreads; (7) stressing about child-related financial problems; and (8) learning that her boyfriend cannot be trusted to stay faithful or marry her. That sounds like a hate-love relationship with the baby on the mother's side and a depressing and anxiety-filled start for any youngster.

Birth mothers may deny ever contemplating abortion. Not all are telling the truth. Thao, the woman who hid her pregnancy for eight months, told me later that she had never considered abortion. However, to others, before and after that time, she admitted to having repeatedly sought money from the drug dealer for that very purpose.

Some birth mothers have spoken of the love they directed to their child in the uterus before the adoption. If feelings and emotions get through to a fetus, it was exposed to and felt that love. However, it makes no sense that only love gets through.

In many cases the child was also exposed in utero to the mother's denial of his existence; the mother's feelings of fear, shame, hurt, and betrayal; and the mother's wishing him dead and trying to kill him. Thus, a baby still in the womb could feel abandoned, unwanted, insecure, sad, angry, and unable to trust even his mother. Not surprisingly, too many teenagers who were adopted soon after birth feel the same way.

Skeptics may deny any link between the teenage feelings and the time in the uterus because those teens cannot consciously remember that time. However, neither can they consciously recall their infancy (including leaving the original mother). Thus, if the skeptics are right, the primal wound theory also falls.

Regardless, my volunteer work taught me that many infants in the neonatal ward, including "preemies" who should not yet have been born, already have a personality and a definite approach to life. These babies (such as the howler, the cheery one, the placid one, the stubborn one, and the withdrawn one) have their own usual way of dealing with the world. Furthermore, some women say they got a preview of what their offspring would be like from how it acted (e.g., constantly kicking) in the uterus.

Studies confirm that human beings can and do learn before birth. According to research, a baby at birth can recognize his mother's voice, the theme song of a television show she watched frequently during pregnancy, a children's rhyme she often recited while pregnant, etc. Clearly, fetuses learn from both good and bad experiences (e.g., soothing music versus loud noises). Also clearly, infants recall some things learned in the womb.

Furthermore, humans may, consciously or unconsciously, retain fetal memories past infancy. According to Nancy Verrier herself, evidence exists of people being able to remember, through hypnosis, attempted abortions.

Moreover, a growing body of research supports the view that too much stress on an expectant mother can, as our ancestors knew, have negative consequences for her fetus. (This is true even in cases where the child stays with his genetic mother, i.e., for a child with or without the so-called "primal wound.") Studies indicate that <u>excessive maternal stress during pregnancy can have adverse effects - including physical, mental, emotional, and behavioral effects - on the child even years later</u>. That stress can be linked to, among other conditions, depression, anxiety, behavioral problems, emotional problems, learning problems, and Attention Deficit/Hyperactivity Disorder - conditions often found in adopted children. In other words, researchers relate to prenatal stress various conditions Ms. Verrier relates to the separation from the biological mother.

Indeed, various teenagers born to and kept by an unwed mother could pass for poster children for the primal wound. They suffer from depression, anxiety, behavioral problems, emotional problems, difficulties in relationships with significant others, etc. Yet, for these teens, the "but for" event causing the primal wound - relinquishment by the birth mother - never occurred!

In any event, getting pregnant young, unmarried, unable to support oneself, and semi-educated is a recipe for a drama-filled pregnancy. The primal wound theory provides some helpful insights. However, it predates much of the research on fetal learning and the dangers of a stressful pregnancy and is too simplistic. As discussed above, a fetus learns from good and bad experiences in the uterus, a preemie who should still be in utero can already have a personality and his own approach to life, an infant has prenatal memories, and a traumatic pregnancy can adversely impact a child in the womb and for years afterward in physical and non-physical ways. In short, a newborn is by no means a blank slate. Pregnancy under traumatic circumstances can have negative effects on the child after birth, whether or not that child remains with his first mother (i.e., despite no primal wound).

ROMANCE AND THE ADOPTED CHILD[25]

Romance may come early or late to an adopted child. Pre-adoption experiences and societal expectations can affect his romantic life. As shown below, the results are unpredictable--and often charming. Here is a glimpse into the romantic life of three adoptees.[26]

Fawn

Many children were adopted by a person of another race or ethnicity. Some, like Fawn, grew up among people who looked different from them. Particularly in the past, these children were likely to face prejudice with regard to dating or marriage.

A Caucasian woman talked to me about this problem. Decades ago, she adopted Fawn, a Native American. According to the woman, her friends had told her not to adopt because the girl would never get married.

In time, Fawn proved the bigoted friends wrong. She did not marry a local boy, perhaps due to prejudice. However, she did succeed in finding a husband. Fawn married an English nobleman!

Jack

Often children awaiting adoption had a variety of foster mothers or orphanage caretakers. A child accustomed from a

---

[25] "Romance" was first published in 2013.

[26] All children's names in this article are pseudonyms to protect privacy.

young age to transient relationships may have difficulty forming a deep attachment and a lasting marriage in later years. At least in his youth, he may continue the pattern of multiple relationships--sometimes with amusing consequences.

Jack was adopted as a one-year-old from Latin America. He came from an orphanage and from foster care. Prior to the adoption, he had experienced at least six moves and six changes in his primary caretaker.

A summary of Jack's social life reveals numerous relationships and frequent change. Perhaps due to all the farewells in his early life and his personality (as well as to his dashing looks), he has had more girlfriends and "best" friends than the average boy.

Jack's romantic life began early. He was one when he got his first girlfriend. Tiffany, a blonde older woman, was two. They met at play school. When he arrived on school mornings, she would run to him bringing him a toy and calling his name.

It was a delightful romance. One day Jack and his classmates were walking hand in hand to the playroom. Tiffany broke away and sprinted to reserve the prized hobby horse for Jack. She helped her tippy little beau to mount. Then he rocked merrily, with Tiffany facing him and both children holding the horse's handles. Another day Jack was racing around and around a pole, with Tiffany in pursuit. Failing to catch him, she stopped, waited for him to complete the circle, and pounced. Then she hugged and kissed him.

Unlike Tiffany, Jack indiscriminately hugged and kissed his playmates. However, he kept forgetting the puckering-up part of the kiss.

Naturally, this toddler romance did not always go smoothly. Jack once went to play school sucking a pacifier attached to his shirt. Tiffany also wanted to suck on the pacifier. When he refused to share, she knocked him down.

After she moved away, Jack had other girlfriends. At this stage the girls took the lead. Jack himself seemed to love everybody.

He was two when he first chased a girl. Leila, a brunette, was a smart, spunky tomboy. One day the teacher wrote in Jack's daily parent report, "Jack displayed his affectionate side today by plastering Leila with kisses. They interact with each other very well." Another day the teacher wrote, "All the kids, especially Leila, really like him."

Unfortunately, this romance provoked jealousy and revenge. A lady-like blonde had a crush on Jack. The boy once altered his practice of playing with everybody to spend the day with Leila. The blonde, incensed, kept eyeing the merry couple as the day progressed. Late that afternoon she went behind Jack--and bit him. At bedtime his shoulder still bore the imprint of all of her teeth.

He remained popular as a three-year-old. Three teachers named him as their favorite pupil. A daily parent report said, "[A] number of new parents have come in asking who Jack is because their children have come home raving about him." According to the play-school director, Jack was the darling of the school.

At four Jack tended to have a crush on multiple girls. Some of them were beautiful, some were not, but all were spunky and intelligent.

When he was five, a boy and a girl invited him to separate birthday parties for the same day. Jack accepted the girl's invitation. The only male invited, he played happily with seven females.

At that age Jack planned to have four wives simultaneously and sixteen children. He picked the prospective brides from his schoolmates. The four-bride roster varied from time to time that year and included girls of different shapes and races. Typically, the common denominator for the brides was spunk and intelligence.

While still five, Jack spent a week at a foreign Club Med. Most of the children vacationing there did not speak English. Because Jack was so outgoing, a hostess-teacher sent shy children from any country to play with him. He soon had a "fan club" of boys, despite the language barrier. Two pretty girls also followed him about the grounds. It was not uncommon to hear, when Jack walked by, a child telling a parent something like, "C'est mon ami, celui-là!"

At night the Club Med guests danced under the stars. Jack's black sneakers had small red lights that flashed in the dimness when he danced. He performed twirls, cartwheels, round-offs, and other gymnastics on the dance floor. The child won several awards that vacation, including the medal for King of the Disco. By the end of the week, the chief of the club, the staff, the French guests, the German guests, and everybody else seemed to know Jack.

When he was six, he liked older women, and they liked him. That summer his main beach romance was a chubby, spunky eleven-year-old. To appear older, Jack claimed to be seven. He often played on the sand with a bunch of college students. He seemed to be their mascot and buddy.

Jack is now eight and still popular. He clearly likes the idea of numerous relationships. Recently, someone asked him how many girlfriends he has. Jack replied, "Two thousand."

Robin

Two children may experience similar conditions prior to adoption. Yet the pattern of their post-adoption relationships may differ markedly.

Robin was adopted from Central America when he was eight months old. Like Jack, he had been in an orphanage and in foster care and had experienced at least six moves and six changes in his primary caretaker. Unlike Jack, Robin shows remarkable constancy in his social life.

He started play school at about ten months old. There he met Will and Cindy. Will was Robin's age, and Cindy, who was in another class, was a month younger. The two boy babies promptly became friends. Soon Will was Robin's best non-family friend.

Since the boys were buddies, they had a joint party at school for their first birthday. It was a soggy celebration. Robin cried and then settled down placidly to his bottle and cake. Shy Will wept through the entire party.

Shortly after Robin turned one, he entered the class for walking toddlers. Will and Cindy were also in the class. At that time Robin basically could not talk. Nonetheless, it soon became clear to the staff that Will was Robin's best friend and Cindy was Robin's girlfriend.

Robin and his classmates enjoyed lolling with their bottles on bean-bag chairs, looking like baby Neros at a party. They could have the bottles only at scheduled times. In part because children had been grabbing random bottles from the refrigerator, the school had added a so-called "lock." This fastener kept out the tots. One day when Robin was at most seventeen months old, he decided it was bottle time.

What followed amazed the teachers. Robin walked to the refrigerator, undid the fastener, and opened the door. He selected, out of more than ten baby bottles, his girlfriend's bottle and his own. He gave Cindy hers and pushed her gently onto a bean bag. Then he reclined on another bean bag, and they enjoyed their drinks together.

Robin and Will celebrated their second birthdays in another joint party. The boys continued to be best friends. Both toddlers had a crush on Cindy. She played with both but clearly preferred Robin.

When Robin was three, a teacher wrote in the daily parent report, "Robin had fun sitting beside Cindy during music class. The two spent much of their time cuddling, not singing." That year he said he was going to marry Cindy and another classmate. Cindy was still smitten with him. She often talked approvingly at home about his beautiful black hair.

Later that year Robin again announced that he was going to marry Cindy. She had kissed him that day, apparently for the first time. He said simply, "Cindy kissed me on the cheek. It made me very happy."

At the time of the kiss, the two three-year-olds had been sweethearts for more than two years. Robin and Will had been best friends longer than Robin and Cindy had been sweethearts, and Will had long had a crush on Cindy. The three children were together constantly in play school and were jokingly called "the three musketeers."

Time brought tests of Robin's commitment to Cindy. After he turned five, he and Will moved without Cindy to another class. Two cute classmates, one a strawberry-blonde Irish-American and the other a raven-haired African-American, often greeted Robin at school. Upon his arrival, the two girls would rush over and hug him. If the strawberry-blonde saw him in the neighborhood pool, she would throw her arms around his waist and hang on until shower time. (Robin would paddle on, seemingly oblivious of the human barnacle.) Yet Cindy remained his sweetheart.

Then, shortly before turning six, he entered the stage of not liking girls. To tease him, his older sibling claimed that Robin had 100 girlfriends and posted the number 100 above the boy's bed. Robin tearfully denied having any and insisted that Cindy was no longer his girlfriend.

Robin is now six. The star of his soccer team, he twice

scored nine goals in a game. Recently, Cindy heard about the two games. She announced that she wanted to see him score nine goals and showed up with her mother at his next match. In the last minute of the game, Robin again scored his ninth goal!

The boy is the darling of several girls and has close friends. Although he, Will, and Cindy attend three different schools and rarely see each other, Robin went to the party for the sixth birthday of Will, who remains his best friend. Robin also attended Cindy's sixth birthday party. Afterward he said that she is still his girlfriend.

Due to all the good-byes in his early life, his personality, or both, Robin is a boy who knows how to hold on. He shows a constancy in romance and friendship rare in such a young child. If the pattern holds, he may one day become, for the woman he marries and their children, a loyal and steadfast family man.

Conclusion

What do adopted children want from romance? Perhaps Omar Khayyam found the answer to this mystery. Some want a jug of wine, a loaf of bread--and thou. However, others prefer a can of soda, a loaf of bread--and thou and thou and thou and thou!

GOOD-BYE AND THE ADOPTED CHILD[27]

Nobody waved good-bye. . . . There were too many good-byes. . . . I wish I could have said good-bye to her. For many adopted children, "good-bye" is a dirty word.

Farewells are painful to them for various reasons. Some of the children were or feel abandoned by a birth parent. Some left more than five foster homes. Some moved from an orphanage to another country with no opportunity to say good-bye to their playmates or a special adult.

The problem is being addressed to some extent. Public employees are reducing the time people spend in foster care before adoption. Social workers, foster parents, and adoptive parents are working together to ease the transition to adoptive homes. For example, a child in foster care may spend several weekends in his proposed adoptive home prior to moving there. Before the move, loving foster parents may say that they will miss him but that the adoption will be good for him. A child in a foreign orphanage may receive photographs of his prospective American family. A child removed from his abusive birth parents may, with help from his adoptive mother, continue to see his birth grandparents.

Unfortunately, the farewells are still a disaster for many youngsters. After one devastating good-bye or multiple good-byes, some adopted children appear to be incapable of caring about anyone. Others turn indiscriminately to

---

[27] "Good-Bye" was first published in 2000.

acquaintances for love. Some run away from home repeatedly (as if to reject their adoptive parents before the parents can reject them). Others become clingy or have trouble leaving home after reaching adulthood. The stories of Sam,[28] Kim, and Jack illustrate some effects of traumatic good-byes.

<u>Sam</u>

Sam needs to know the whereabouts of his parents and has problems with good-byes. There are reasons for his insecurity. Sam was born in Korea. When he was little, his birth mother repeatedly sneaked out and left him home alone for hours. Then, when he was five, she claimed that she had arranged for him to visit his birth father in the United States. In fact, she had arranged for her son to be adopted by a childless American couple. The boy said good-bye to her believing that he would soon return home. Thus, Sam at a young age had learned that a parent could suddenly disappear without warning, that a parent could not be trusted, and that a parent's "au revoir" could mean "good-bye."

When Sam arrived in America, his adoptive parents had to deal with the falsehoods. Eventually, he began to believe that his parents would not walk out on him.

When Sam was about nine, the parents decided to adopt again. The couple, who no longer qualified for a Korean adoption, switched to Russia for a girl.

---

[28] Except for Emily Dickinson, all names in this article were changed.

Sam's mother planned to travel alone to Russia. Before saying good-bye, she promised him she would return. Unfortunately, problems in Russia extended the trip. For over a month the boy was without his mother. They talked occasionally by telephone. After a while he began to deny it was her on the phone. Sam announced that his mother had died and, despite the phone calls, insisted she was dead.

Finally, the mother returned with four-year-old Katya. Sam was handsome, black-haired, and tall. Katya was pretty, blonde, and petite.

From the start, Sam wanted to get rid of his little sister, and Katya was crazy about her big brother. To his anger, she tagged along after him. He decapitated her prized Barbie doll. She cried but continued to follow him about. Over and over he said the same offensive things to her. Grateful for any attention from him and not understanding his English, she would respond adoringly, "Sam! Sam!"

He would say to his sister, "I hate you, Katya. Dad hates you. Mom hates you. Everybody here hates you, Katya. Go back to Russia."

Katya would reply adoringly, "Sam! Sam!"

The trip to Russia hurt the relationship between Sam and his family. He rejected his parents, apparently no longer believing in their love for him. Though the boy was in emotional pain, he refused to let himself be loved by anyone. Sam's mother was heartsick. She feared that by adopting a second child she had lost her first.

Kim

It is possible for a child to be scarred by a single devastating good-bye. Kim is an example.

I heard of Kim from her adoptive mother. Kim was born in the Orient. To some Asians, girls are expendable. One day a relative took her to a big city she had never seen before. He led the girl to a park bench, directed her to wait for him, and abandoned her there. Because she could not explain where she lived, that was her last contact with her birth family.

Eventually, an American couple learned about Kim. They already had a large foster and adoptive family. They had taken in other hard-knocks children and were willing to add one more.

Kim started school shortly after arriving in the United States. The building was miles from her new home via a complicated route. One of her new relatives drove her to the schoolyard, which Kim had never seen before. The relative instructed her to wait to be picked up after school.

When the person meeting Kim arrived, later than intended, at the school, the girl was nowhere to be found. Family members fanned out looking everywhere for her. It was a frantic search, because Kim was a stranger to the United States, could not speak basic English, and did not know her new address in any language.

Suddenly, Kim showed up alone on her doorstep. It turned out that she had developed a method for never being abandoned again. During her one ride to school, Kim had memorized the way home.

<u>Jack</u>

111

Some adopted children bear the emotional scars of too many good-byes. Jack is an example.

When the boy was adopted at age one from a foreign orphanage, he was suffering from malnutrition and too many changes in caretaker. His brunette hair had a reddish tint, his skin was sickly pale, and his body was very thin except for a distended belly. He also had temporarily lost his ability to walk. Although he weighed less than when walking, his legs could no longer support his weight.

Prior to adoption, Jack had been in and out of an orphanage and foster care. Perhaps for this reason, his emotional attachments seemed indiscriminate and shallow. During his first few years in the United States, he appeared to love virtually everybody, including strangers.

Jack did show some preferences, particularly for his new father and paternal grandfather. The night he met the grandfather, he seemed to recognize instantly the similarity between the two men.

When Jack was about seventeen months old, he learned to wave good-bye and to open doors by turning the doorknob. Subsequently, the father had to leave for his first overnight trip since the boy's arrival.

Jack's parents took him to the airport, to give him as much time as possible with his dad. It was a mistake. When Jack saw the suitcase and his father waving good-bye, he began crying. His mother could not get through to him that his dad would return. During the drive from the airport, he wept in a way he never had before. The toddler seemed to be in mourning, with a grief of an adult intensity.

When they were nearly home, the mother recalled Jack's immediate recognition of the similarity between his father and grandfather. She turned the car around and drove through the dark to the grandparents' house. The weeping child did draw comfort from his grandfather.

After the tears stopped, Jack initiated a chilling game. He walked to the room adjoining the one in which his mother and grandparents were seated and closed the door. Then he opened the door, waved good-bye to them, and slammed the door shut. He seemed to be rejecting his relatives and practicing for the future. Over and over the child, still red-eyed from crying, went through the routine of opening the door, giving a fake smile, waving good-bye, and then slamming the door. In his brief life he had been taken away from or abandoned by various people. Through the game, it was finally Jack's turn to decide when to say good-bye.

A Respectful Good-Bye

Regardless of how miserable an adopted child's past life was, he may experience pain from the farewell to that life. (To the surprise of many people, a youngster can even miss a birth parent who abused him repeatedly.) The bad things that happened cannot be erased, but they can be put into perspective and loosen their hold on his future. To ease the pain and reduce the adverse effects, it helps to give the child a respectful good-bye to the old life. This means a good-bye that respects him and his self-image and that recognizes his birth relatives, birth culture, and birth country as part of his heritage. It is in part an "au revoir" rather than a permanent parting. A respectful good-bye includes some of the following steps:

1. A social worker takes the child from his birth family to a safe place and explains to him what is happening. It is important that the child not feel lied to, tricked, or kidnapped;

2. A social worker acclimates the child to the idea of adoption before introducing the prospective adoptive parents. A poorly prepared child is more likely to try to sabotage the adoption;

3. Before the child's move to the adoptive home, a social worker arranges visits through which the proposed adoptive parents and the child become comfortable with each other. In some cases, the would-be adoptive parents serve first as the child's foster parents, which tests whether they are the right parents for him;

4. For an international adoption, the adoptive parents elect to fly to the child's homeland to pick him up, rather than having him travel with an escort. The parents thus learn firsthand about his daily routines and birth country and accompany him on his journey to the new life;

5. For an international adoption in which an older child does travel to the United States before meeting the adoptive family, the prospective parents send him cheery photographs of their family and home. It is

frightening for a child to leave his native country for a strange land, particularly to join a family of another race sight unseen;

6. The child gets to say good-bye to people dear to him. For what not to do, an organization whisked an eleven-year-old girl away without warning from her Brazilian orphanage for an international adoption. The girl regrets that she could not say good-bye to her best friend and a kind social worker;

7. Someone important to the child waves good-bye and expresses approval of the move as good for the child;

8. The adoptive parent learns about the child's daily routines, likes, and dislikes from his current caretaker and eases his transition to a different life by gradual introduction of new routines;

9. The adoptive parent gives the child time to grieve after the move. In addition, he raises the subject of the child's past life occasionally and makes clear the adoptee is free to talk about it. In discussing the child's birth relatives with him, the adoptive parent is tactful but truthful;

10. The adoptive parent includes photographs or other mementos from the child's past in the family album or a "life book" available to him. That parent also places a photograph of the birth mother or someone else dear to the child in his bedroom. The child decides when to put away the

picture (which may mean years later);

11. The adoptive parent arranges contacts between the child and some significant people from the old life (e.g., a birth sibling living in a different home or a birth parent);

12. Even when the birth family's address is unknown, the adoptive parent accepts that the child may want to see the family again. If the child is mature enough (e.g., at eighteen years old), wishes to locate his birth relatives, and wants assistance in the search, the adoptive parent helps find them;

13. The adoptive parent provides contacts with people and activities of the child's race, ethnicity, or birth country and arranges for him to learn his birth language;

14. After an international adoption, the adoptive parents travel with the child to his birth country for a visit or for family vacations. Although the homeland trip may cause painful flashbacks, it presents an opportunity to confront the past; and

15. The adoptive parent arranges for therapy to help the child deal with past good-byes. Some adoptees need therapy immediately. Others may require it after an event, such as an unwanted breakup with a high school sweetheart, that recalls the anguish of the earlier good-byes.

For many adopted children, the good-bye issues need to be revisited over time. Adoptive parents can help their child by giving him a respectful good-bye to the old life. They can help even more by providing a new life--a life of love and stability.

Where Are They Now?

The boy who claimed his mother had died in Russia is now thirteen. Approximately four years ago, when the mother finally came home with Katya, a wretched period began in which Sam said mean things to the little girl and walled himself off emotionally from his family. About nine months later, the situation vastly improved. Sam accepted his sister and the continuation of his parents' love. At age twelve he put away the photograph of his birth mother that had hung in his bedroom for seven years. However, something stayed the same. Little Katya still adores big Sam.

The girl abandoned on a park bench is now a young adult. The last I heard, Kim could not relax and enjoy the conversation on car rides. She was too busy memorizing the way home.

The malnourished toddler who began grieving at the airport is now eleven. When Jack's parents adopted him, they set out to provide the food, love, and stability he needed so badly. His life since then with his close-knit family has been a mixture of sameness and novelty. Academically, Jack works hard in school and has participated in several programs for gifted students. Emotionally, he still bears scars. However, a homeland trip at age nine helped him to cope with past good-byes. Socially, the boy remains a "people person," reaching out to old and young alike.

Physically, he overcame malnutrition to become a stellar athlete. At age nine he won a presidential National Physical Fitness Award given in his elementary school. Even more surprising, at age ten he won a spot on a youth team chosen for an international soccer tournament. In short, at age eleven Jack has lived in the same neighborhood in the same house with the same parents for a decade--and has played in Europe on the soccer team representing the United States!

Conclusion

There are millions of children in need of a permanent family. According to Emily Dickinson, parting is all we know of heaven and all we need of hell. Too many minors awaiting adoption have repeatedly faced this hell. They deserve better.

SPORTS AND THE ADOPTED CHILD[29]

A "born athlete" may be an adopted athlete. Based on informal surveys, adopted children are over-represented among the better athletes. Some even grow up to be champion of the world.

Dan O'Brien is an example. The man who wins the world championship in decathlon is called the greatest athlete in the world (because decathlon consists of ten different sports). Dan, an American adopted as a toddler, won the championship three times. He also walked away with the decathlon gold medal in the Olympics.

Why adoptees are over-represented among the stellar athletes seems, at first, a total mystery. However, five factors appear to contribute to the athletic success of adopted children as a group. First, the group has a high incidence of Attention Deficit/Hyperactivity Disorder (for which Dan was diagnosed). A hyperactive child has more chance of being a sports star than a sedentary child. Second, the average adoptive parent is richer than the average birth parent. A larger percentage of adoptive parents than of birth parents may be willing to pay for sports camps and private coaching, which make a good athlete better. The stories of four extraordinary athletes point to the three additional factors.

---

[29] "Sports" was first published in 2002.

<u>Jack</u>[30]

Jack was suffering from malnutrition when he was adopted at age one from a foreign country. He came from a Latin American orphanage and foster care. His brunette hair had a reddish tint, his skin was sickly pale, and his body was very thin except for a distended belly. The boy was so weak that he had lost temporarily his ability to walk. Although he had already learned how to walk and weighed less than when walking, his legs could no longer support him.

Jack also bore emotional scars. Perhaps because he had experienced too many changes of caretaker, his emotional attachments seemed indiscriminate and shallow. He appeared to love almost everyone, including strangers.

The adoptive parents set out to provide the food, love, and stability their new child needed so badly. They made long-term and short-term plans for his welfare. One plan concerned their dwelling, which was a "starter home" for young families with limited finances. The parents decided that their son would stay in the same neighborhood in the same house for a minimum of five years.

Jack is now eleven. His life with his closely knit family has been a mixture of sameness and novelty. Academically, he works hard in school and has been in several programs for gifted students. Emotionally, he still bears scars. However, a homeland trip at age nine helped him to cope with the past. Socially, he remains a "people person" who often talks to

---

[30] The name of this child was changed to protect his identity.

strangers.

Financially, life improved. This family could have moved to a much nicer home.

Physically, Jack overcame malnutrition to become a star athlete. Two years in a row in elementary school he won a presidential National Physical Fitness Award. Even more surprising, at age ten the boy won a spot on a youth team chosen for an international soccer tournament. He was the youngest and littlest child to qualify.

In short, at age eleven Jack has lived in the same neighborhood in the same house with the same parents for a decade. He has also played in Europe on the soccer team representing the United States!

Scott Hamilton

Adopted athletes can be found in every sport. Some love basketball, a team sport played in the summer Olympics. Scott Hamilton preferred an individual sport of the winter Olympics.

Scott was born in the United States and adopted in infancy. He soon exhibited major medical problems. He did not grow at all for a few years. In elementary school he was always the smallest child in the class, and he wore a feeding tube, inserted in him for food supplements through his nose. At one stage he was expected to die within six months.

When Scott was a frail nine-year-old, he went to an ice rink. He liked what he saw and began skating regularly, with his feeding tube trailing behind. The cold air and exercise agreed with him. He became strong and vigorous, though of small stature.

Scott's parents encouraged his interest in skating, which had helped cure him. To pay for his expensive lessons, they sold their home and moved to a cheaper one. Even after his dear mother grew ill from cancer, she helped him as best she could. To his sorrow, she died when he was eighteen, before he became famous.

Scott reached the top in men's figure skating. As an amateur, he won four world championships and an Olympic gold medal. As a professional, he won the world professional competition twice. His mother would have been proud of him. Scott proved to be a classy, admired, and much loved champion.

Surya Bonaly

Adopted females win gold medals, too. For example, Kitty Carruthers won, with her brother (also adopted), the United States championship in pairs figure skating four times. Ashia Hansen, who was adopted in infancy, became a world champion in triple jump. Fatima Whitbread, adopted at age fourteen, won the world championship in javelin.

Surya Bonaly, an all-around athlete, had the potential to win gold medals in various winter and summer sports. Of African descent, she was born in France and adopted at a young age by a Caucasian French couple.

Growing up, Surya excelled in both indoor and outdoor events. She became the female world junior figure skating champion. According to public sources, she also competed at the international level in tumbling, trampoline, and diving.

Eventually, Surya began to concentrate on skating. The Bonalys had their home in the South of France and were not rich. However, the best opportunities for a French skater were in the capital. Therefore, the family trundled from the South to Paris, so Surya could train under a coach there. The coach was quoted as saying about the Bonalys, "For a year they lived in a truck" with their dogs.

Life was not easy in other respects for Surya. It must have been difficult growing up a black child in a white society. It was also hard, with her sturdy, muscular build and unorthodox skating style and costumes, to become a champion in a sport that prized sylph-like beauty and orthodoxy.

Surya worked long hours for fame in women's figure skating, with her parents' support. Her father quit his job to become her agent, and her mother became her coach. The couple made numerous sacrifices for their daughter. By the end of her amateur career, Surya had won the championship of France nine times and the championship of Europe five times. This exciting and popular skater had succeeded against great odds.

Greg Louganis

Many adopted athletes show their fighting spirit at a young age. However, Greg Louganis at a young age was giving up. With his self-destructive acts and problems, he was an unlikely prospect for sports glory.

Of Samoan and European ancestry, Greg was born in the United States. His adoptive parents met him when he was nine months old and in foster care.

Like many future Olympic champions, the boy had a difficult childhood. He had the learning impediment dyslexia (not diagnosed until his college days), was homosexual, and had dark coloring. Children at school called him "retard," "sissy," and "nigger" and occasionally beat him up. As a teenager, Greg was sometimes drunk and used illegal drugs. He also suffered from depression. Desperately unhappy, he tried several times to kill himself.

Greg turned for refuge to his mother and athletics. He came to realize that his mother loved him despite his failures. She scrimped and saved to pay for his sports expenses and tried to shield him from his authoritarian, hard-drinking father. With her help, the boy escaped his troubles for part of each day through physical activities.

Eventually, Greg decided to focus on diving. He began his Olympic career at age sixteen and ended it at twenty-eight. In between he won hundreds of championships, including world championships, in springboard and platform diving. During those years he was injured in diving accidents and began medical treatment for the Human Immunodeficiency Virus. Yet he forged on in his sport.

In the life of this athlete, what stands out most is his last Olympics. It was, from beginning to end, a death-defying test of fighting spirit.

The contest started with the springboard diving competition, which opened with an eleven-round elimination match the day before the finals. Greg, though threatened by a deadly disease, was competing. In the ninth round of the elimination match, he leaped off the diving board, spun in the air backward, and hit the board headfirst. Greg fell into the pool and was led away bleeding. Refusing to give up, he returned about thirty-five minutes later, with stitches in his head, to finish the match.

Before the accident, the young man had planned to perform that very dive in the finals. When the moment arrived, he was scared, but he forced himself to do it! To the delight of the crowd, he won the springboard gold medal.

The Olympic platform diving competition began less than a week later. Going into the concluding round, Greg was in second place. When the time came for his last jump, he climbed to the platform high above the pool. Steeling himself, he launched into the Dive of Death. The hardest dive of all, it was not in the front-runner's Olympic program and was notorious for killing a man. Greg captured the platform gold medal with the Dive of Death.

It is not clear whether this competitor became a great diver in spite of his problems or because of them. However, he set the standard for athletes in his field. According to A Who's Who of Sports Champions, Greg was "the greatest diver in history."

Conclusion

The four extraordinary athletes are different and alike. The variable factors within the group include sex, race, age, and size. They also include the child's country of birth and adoptive country and whether the adoption was international, transracial, of an infant, and from an orphanage. Yet there is a common denominator. Each athlete: (1) had survived hard times; (2) was adopted and backed by at least one staunchly committed adoptive parent; and (3) became a fighter, showing the heart of a champion.

These three factors help explain the victories of the four athletes (and the sports success of adopted children as a group). The hard times shaped the athletes' character and left them in some ways stronger.

The committed adoptive parent provided emotional support--and much more--and made sacrifices many parents would not make. After all, to provide sports lessons to a child, how many people would trade in their home for a cheaper one or live in a truck?

However, the crucial factor was becoming a fighter. Victims of adverse circumstances, the four athletes rejected the role of victim. All four are heroes, for what they overcame to reach their sports success. Jack, because of his fighting spirit and great heart, went from having been crippled by malnutrition to racing around a soccer field in international competition. Scott transformed himself from a sickly nine-year-old skating with a feeding tube to a world champion on ice. Surya overcame racial prejudice and triumphed as a nonconformist in a sport that rewarded conformity. Finally, there is Greg. Ridiculed, dyslexic, and suicidal, he turned into the greatest diver who ever lived.

So I have a message for adopted youngsters competing in soccer, the Special Olympics, or another sporting event.

According to Merle Shain, there are only two ways to approach life--as a victim or as a gallant fighter. Some of you suffered hard times. Yet many of you still strive to be a good sport and to do your best in athletics and in life. Three cheers for being such gallant fighters!

RACE AND CLASS AND
THE ADOPTED CHILD[31]

Adoption usually changes the status of a child. Often his original parents were at a lower social, economic, and educational level than his new parents (particularly in international adoptions). In many cases a baby born to a young, unwed minority woman is raised by an older, married white couple. The changed circumstances can make a difference in how the child is treated in a world where race and class still matter.

An adopted child's real ethnicity counts less than his perceived ethnicity in determining how he gets treated. Strangers draw conclusions about ethnic background. (Thus, one Hispanic boy was variously viewed as Hispanic, Caucasian, Native American, African-American, and Asian.) These conclusions, correct or not, may lead people to misjudge the socioeconomic status (i.e., class) of the child and his household. For example, some whites assume they rank higher class-wise than a black youth--until they discover his adoptive parents are also white or have professional degrees.

Someone prejudiced against a race or class may discriminate against an adopted child considered part of that group. This can cause problems (such as obstacles to academic success, unfair stereotypes, insults, police

---

[31] "Race" was first published in 2012.

misconduct, discriminatory punishment, and even danger) for the victim. Below is a discussion of these pitfalls and of how some adoptees--or their champions--dealt with the bigots.

<u>Obstacles to Academic Success</u>

A report card helps determine whether a student will get into a good college or even attend one. Some teachers have low expectations for minority students and grade accordingly, as illustrated by the story of Robin.[32]

Robin was adopted as an infant from Central America by an upper-middle-class Caucasian couple. He is smart, as most of his grades indicate. However, one year in high school, he kept bringing home C's in English.

A meeting occurred between Robin's mother and the English teacher. The teacher was surprised to see a white mom, to hear that Robin liked the assigned book <u>Of Mice and Men,</u> and to learn that he would enter college after graduation (although he was on the honor roll at a school where almost everyone goes on to higher education). The mother left convinced that the woman, because of Robin's ethnicity, had assumed that he was from a poor minority family, was incapable of appreciating a John Steinbeck novel, and was going nowhere. After the meeting, Robin's grades in the class turned, as if by magic, into A's and B's.

Sometimes the root of the problem lies outside the

---

[32] All names of adoptees in this article are aliases for privacy reasons.

classroom. One high school administrator (who retired recently) hated children of color. He worked with notable success over several decades at "persuading" minority students to drop out of school. As part of his harassment campaign, he told the teacher of a well-behaved Asian boy having trouble with Spanish, "Give him the lowest grade possible."

The man especially despised people of mixed race. He said to the adoptive parent of a biracial student, "[Y]ou are lucky we let . . . [your child into this place], since . . . [the child] is mixed."

Unfair Stereotypes

While Robin was hurt by a negative stereotype, Matt was troubled by a positive one. The teenager, who was adopted from Korea, shines in English courses but struggles with math. This confounds teachers who expect every student of Asian descent to excel with numbers. Matt resents being chided for failure to live up to the stereotype.

A shocking incident (e.g., the shooting rampage by a Virginia Tech college student on campus) can lead to the typecasting of minority youths. If someone of their ethnic background commits a horrendous act, others may consider the youths likewise capable of that act. Teasing is the mildest form of this racial targeting.

Matt had little in common with the Virginia Tech gunman but a Korean homeland. Yet soon after the massacre, this adoptee was quizzed on the subject at school before the whole class. A boy, after establishing Matt's country of birth, asked, "So are you going to shoot us all?"

Matt won the round and the laughing support of his classmates with his reply. He said, "No, but if I did, I'd shoot you first!"

Insults

Some adopted children face public insults. This happened to Sam.

One day Sam, who is partly Asian, was entering an autobus. A female passenger objected. She announced that "people like that" should not be allowed on the bus. Not even the driver came to the boy's defense.

Sam, furious, told the woman off. The incident ended with Sam on board and the segregationist in tears.

Often the insults are silent, though the meaning is clear. For example, some salespeople follow minority children, including adoptees, around the store, considering them more likely to steal than white children.

The affronts can be indirect but painful nonetheless. For instance, a business that assigns white employees to deal with the public and gives black employees the menial backup jobs sends a clear message to black customers, including adoptees.

Occasionally the insults come from a surprising source. An American family was staying at a nice hotel in Colombia, the country from which the children had been adopted years before. One day the son and daughter set forth from their lodging. When they failed to return on time, the parents grew worried. The boy and girl were found waiting outside. The doorman, certain they could not be guests of such an upscale hotel, had barred them from the building. Yet he and the children were of the same ethnicity!

The insults can be ongoing. For example, a teenaged adoptee, who tans deeply, repeatedly found himself the target of pointed stares when with his lighter-skinned girlfriend.

Indeed, a couple perceived to be interracial may encounter more than glares and poor service at business establishments. In one horrific incident, Jack, a college student adopted from Latin America, was attacked by three James Madison University students. He was leaving the apartment of his white girlfriend when the goons struck. This young man, whose hobbies include weight lifting, is very strong. Despite getting knocked down and kicked in the face, he fought back with fury. Jack broke the nose of one of his assailants and scared them off. The next day he and ten friends tracked down the three thugs in their residence. While the trio cowered, their visitors, without ever touching them, taught them a lesson they will never forget.

Some law-abiding adoptees assume a menacing persona. They try to conform, in clothing and manner, to the gangster stereotype for their ethnic group. The explanation for this mysterious behavior is unclear. The tough-guy role could be a response to too many insults, since even racists are wary of provoking such angry-looking youths.

Police Misconduct

Too often the insults come from policemen and constitute unfair police harassment--or worse. Jack, the Latino college student, received an automobile as a gift from his adoptive parents for his high school graduation. Subsequently, the car was stopped repeatedly by police officers in several states. Once lawmen actually dismantled parts of the vehicle in a lengthy and vain search for illegal drugs. In the worldview of some policemen, if a young Hispanic male is driving an expensive-looking Volvo, he either stole it or bought it with drug money.

The police often mistreat minorities, including adoptees. Last night law officers showed up at a birthday party. They picked certain guests for a breathalyzer test, which nobody failed. Although most of the partiers were white, the test was administered only to guests of other races. (The blacks were not surprised.) An adoptee was in the group targeted. He was neither driving nor under the drinking age, but he was subjected to the test in front of his friends anyway.

Many Americans were taught to view a policeman as "Officer Friendly." One of them (the Caucasian mother of the minority adoptee subjected to the breathalyzer test) has modified her views after a series of events. Among other incidents, a lawman aimed his gun at her non-threatening son during a routine traffic stop, and another time a lawman handcuffed her son temporarily for no known crime. Increasingly, the woman believes that a policeman is her friend and her child's enemy.

Discriminatory Punishment

Sometimes punishment or harsher punishment is reserved for minorities, including adoptees. This happened to a Latino boy adopted by a white couple.

One day Kenny and his friends got into mischief in elementary school. All the troublemakers were Caucasian except him. The administrators decided to make an example of someone. Although the Hispanic child had acted no worse than his buddies, he alone was to be disciplined.

His mother refused to accept this blatant discrimination. According to her argument, Kenny should be considered white because he had white parents, lived in a white neighborhood, and attended a white school. The administration backed down on the punishment.

<u>Danger!</u>

Bigots can be dangerous when they judge adoptees based on skin color or perceived status in society. For example, racists may, like the James Madison students (see above), turn into a pack of violent savages, may point a loaded gun (see above), or may make false accusations of illegal behavior.

As earlier noted, Robin was adopted as a baby from Central America. He and his friends are good kids. When he was a sophomore in high school, he was an honor-roll scholar, wrestled on the varsity team, and won a student-athlete award. Yet that year the assistant principal of a rival high school accused the teenager of a gang-related crime.

At the time wrestlers were competing in a district tournament to determine who would qualify for the regional meet. Robin fought his opponent from the host high school for a regional slot and won.

Then a picture was taken of the finalists. In the pose, Robin's hands were positioned in an unusual way.

Immediately afterward the white assistant principal of the host school pulled the boy aside. He announced that Robin was going to be arrested and imprisoned!

The assistant principal claimed the student had flashed a gang sign in the photograph. The man could not identify the gang. (Nor could he rely on clothing, jewelry, or tattoos to corroborate the charge because the boy was dressed in his team uniform, wore no jewelry, and is not tattooed.) Yet he was sure about the sign, due to the unexpected position of the hands of a Latino youth. A bully, he gave the youth no chance to explain.

Robin's coach, a dignified black man, tried unsuccessfully to handle the tense situation. With the accuser still insisting on the police and jail, the coach dispatched one of his wrestlers to locate Robin's dad.

Standard attire for parents at wrestling matches consists of jeans and a tee shirt or sweatshirt. Robin's father, a Caucasian lawyer who had come to the tournament directly from court, strode up wearing a dark business suit, white shirt, and tie.

The man, outraged, resolved the conflict on the spot. At his demand and with the concurrence of the school's principal, the standoff ended with the assistant principal apologizing to Robin and to his coach for the false accusation.

When the father and the coach were out of earshot of the

group, the dad, in explanation, said, "I'm very white."

The coach, laughing, replied, "You figured it out!"

However, relative class power also played a role in the school's total capitulation. At the sight of Robin's father, the accuser's expression had changed to that of a bully realizing he is sorely outmatched.

In the dad's view, no educational institution serious about retaining and graduating its minority students should employ an administrator like the accuser. The next day he called the principal from the night before. He also contacted a friend on the school board. The school system did not renew the assistant principal's contract.

Conclusion

Despite the election of an African-American president, a child's perceived race and perceived class continue to affect how he is treated. Sometimes minority children, including adoptees, are the target of ugly discrimination. To get equal treatment, the victims should not have to qualify (under the test of Kenny's mother) as honorary white people. In short, all parents should, like Robin's father, help fight bigotry.

As Robin's story, still unfolding, shows, there is also something the targets of the discrimination can do. They can refuse to allow the racist views to determine who they are. Early in high school Robin was, in the eyes of an intolerant stranger and a biased teacher, either a gangster or going nowhere. However, others see him more clearly. Later in high school he received the Gentleman Award (including a certificate calling him "an all-around good guy"). When this teenager was a senior, he was courted by various universities. He is now a freshman at a college of science.

HUMOR AND THE ADOPTED CHILD[33]

It is hard to be a good parent. Depending on circumstances, a parent should be like yin or yang (e.g., firm or flexible, stern or gentle, and sharp-eared or selectively deaf). A jolly child tends to be more cooperative than an angry one. Therefore, good humor often works better than punishment as a parental response. To quote an imaginary fortune cookie, "Confucius says, 'A man who is serious about being a good parent learns to use humor.'"

Defined broadly, "good humor" can be found in incongruity (e.g., a nun dancing the Charleston), absurdity, silliness, jokes, games, playfulness, fun activities, unusual conditions, and mundane circumstances. Good humor is also a mindset. It makes life cheerier and has physiological benefits.

Humor can play an important role in raising an adopted child. Specifically, it can be used: (1) to reach an understanding of fun for someone who does not know what fun is and to develop a joint definition of fun for the parent and child; (2) to achieve another short-term goal (e.g., defusing a tense situation); and (3) to achieve a long-term goal (e.g., building a lasting attachment between the parent and child). Real-life examples are provided below.

Creating an Understanding of Fun
and a Shared Definition of Fun

---

[33] "Humor" was first published in 2013.

Many newly adopted children survived tough times or differ in background from their adoptive parents. A hard-knocks child may know little about fun (are we having fun yet?), seldom having experienced it. A child from another background may have a different idea of fun from the new parent (e.g., teasing the cat). To the surprise of the adoptive parents, the newcomer may appear impassive or unreceptive when the parents initiate enjoyable activities. Thus, in many adoptive families it is necessary to teach a new member what fun means or to arrive at a joint definition of fun.

To break the ice between the adoptive parent and the new child, the parent can try gentle tickling or good-natured roughhousing. The tickling approach was used with Liza.[34]

Liza was born in Vietnam. During her infancy, she lost both of her parents. Although relatives took her in, they had little time for her. Eventually, she became part of a large American family.

Liza's new father had a bedtime ritual. Every evening he went to the girls' and the boys' bedrooms and tickled each child present in turn. The typical response was giggles. Liza alone remained silent. Night after night the father made the rounds of the children. Suddenly one evening, Liza seemed to grasp that tickling was fun. After that she giggled like her siblings and welcomed the ritual.

A fun activity can evoke a strong negative emotion in a

---

[34] Every child and pet name was changed for this article to safeguard privacy.

new family member. In the case of Jack, the emotion was fear.

Jack was adopted from Latin America at age one. Prior to the adoption, he had spent considerable time in foster and institutional care penned up in a crib. Jack's adoptive parents assumed he would enjoy a playground trip. In fact, he seemed to know nothing about swings and slides and to be timid of them. The toddler was rigid with fear on his first ride in a basket swing.

On the second playground trip, Jack still appeared frightened in the basket. Therefore, his mother put him in the sandbox. He stood there studying the swings. He seemed to be observing that people considered swings good and did not fall off the strange contraptions. On the third trip, Jack finally began to like swing rides.

Sometimes it is the parent who must revise his conception of fun, at least for a while. Robin was adopted as an infant from a Central American orphanage. He loved to sit in his adoptive mother's lap watching everything. He grew wide-eyed at the sight of his dad roughhousing. The father would throw Robin's older brother in the air, catch him, and twirl him around upside down. The brother, gasping with laughter, would beg, "More! More!"

Apparently, preverbal Robin misinterpreted the roughhousing as something dreadful. For nearly three years he basically avoided his dad. Whenever the father tried the exuberant roughhousing that had worked so well with the brother, Robin wailed. The breakthrough turned out to be repeated father-son sessions of quiet, slow-motion roughhousing.

As part of the "Slo-Mo Roughhousing Game," the father would hold Robin aloft for a while near the ceiling. The man would also flip the boy head over heels in slow motion and perform other gentle gymnastics. Over time, as Robin came to realize he was safe in his dad's hands, the father sped up the action and raised the decibel level. Now Robin often pounces on his beloved dad to initiate the spirited play.

<u>Reaching Another Short-Term Goal with Humor</u>

Humor can help a parent to meet other short-term goals (e.g., getting a child to complete that day's chore without an argument). The humor can be planned or extemporaneous. A parent who finds it difficult to be playful may prefer to make preparations in advance.

An impasse between a mother and daughter called for humor with advance planning. The mother was a serious person. The daughter was a teenager adopted from India. The two argued frequently, with each entrenched in her position. Efforts to move things forward by discussion and reasoning failed. Finally, the woman obtained professional advice on how to break the stalemate and made the necessary preparations. During the next dead-end argument, she turned her back. When she finally turned around, her face was covered--by a Halloween mask!

The daughter was startled into silence. To succeed, humor does not necessarily have to elicit laughter. The incongruity of a monster mask on a serious-minded mother

141

derailed the argument and broke the impasse.

Humor may help a child cope with hurt feelings. Two brothers, adopted from Latin America, came home upset from elementary school. A European-American friend had gone up to each boy separately during the day and called him a "Spic."

In response, the boys' dad talked to the father of the offending child. Subsequently, the mom had a conversation, thought out in advance, with her sons. According to her, the name-calling must have made them feel hurt and angry. There is a ridiculous, mean epithet for every ethnic group. The mother explained that these labels are unacceptable because their purpose is to hurt and anger people. She emphasized how ridiculous the slurs sound and gave examples, with the understanding that the boys should not use them. Because the names sounded so silly (e.g., Honkie, Limey, and Frog), the painful conversation ended with the children in giggles.

A silly game can restore harmony to the family. An adoptive mother tucked her son into bed nightly with a kiss. Regardless of his behavior during the day, she wanted the day to conclude on a loving note. One evening the boy became angry at something and refused her kiss. She responded by blowing him a kiss--and deliberately missing him. Her impromptu gesture started the "Flying Kiss Game" and ended with a laughing child and a game they subsequently played for fun.

In this game a blown kiss that misses a child lands

somewhere or ricochets off something. The mother and son first played it when he was in his bedroom with his pets. Because of the woman's "poor aim" or the madly bobbing boy, her kisses flew unpredictably to a landing place disclosed by her. ("Yuck! I just kissed Spot on the lips!" "That kiss bounced off the wall and got you on the left ear." "Oh, gross! I missed you and kissed the lizard!") The game resulted in a feeling of closeness and a merry end to a difficult day.

Reaching a Long-Term Goal with Humor

A parent is not a comedian. Nonetheless, occasional use of humor does make it easier to attain a long-term goal (e.g., building a close-knit family or helping a child who was abused overcome touching problems).

Of the various forms of humor, persistent playfulness may work best on a long-term basis. The parent does not have to do one amusing thing over and over. It is only necessary to be playful on a number of occasions over time. The persistent playfulness approach was used with Jack (discussed above in this article).

The boy was adopted at age one from a foreign orphanage. It had a mortality rate allegedly over 50%. Like many adopted children, Jack exhibited touching problems. Based on what his adoptive parents could uncover, he had received insufficient good touching and had been hit. To complicate these problems, he could not stay still, due to Attention Deficit/Hyperactivity Disorder. The first year after the adoption, Jack's mother generally had to chase him to hug him, and he would soon struggle to keep moving. As for lap-sitting, within ten seconds he would flail around to escape. As for being kissed, he not infrequently would rub off the kiss.

One day, after Jack wiped off his mother's kiss, she started the "Kiss-Off Game." This game converts what otherwise might be rejection of the parent by the child into their shared rejection of a kiss. If Jack rejected her kiss, she would rub it off, try another one, rub it off if it got rejected, and then try again. ("Was this kiss better?" "No." "Then take it away. Was this one better?" "No." "You mean you didn't like my 'wonderful' kiss?!") The game included "good" kisses such as a light smooch on the hair and wonderfully "bad" (i.e., silly) kisses, including a snuffling doggy kiss and a loud "razzberry" kiss. At first the boy rejected all of them, so the mother vigorously rubbed them all away. After playing the game a few times, he began to admit to liking one or two kisses. Jack finally was getting multiple kisses and keeping some, in a joking atmosphere.

Eventually, a new game evolved. This "Good Kiss/Bad Kiss Game" gave the youngster a choice between good and bad kisses. If Jack wiped away or refused his mother's good-bye kiss before leaving the house for school, she would react with mock horror and "threaten" him with a bad kiss. She might say, "Oh, poor child, I feel so sorry for you! You're going to get such a slimy, yucky kiss later. It's your choice-- good kiss now or bad kiss later." Generally Jack, laughing, would run to her for his good kiss. If not, she would pounce on him later, give him a bad kiss, and accept with feigned dismay a bad one in return.

Jack's mother also hugged him as best she could. In addition, she sought help from his play-school teachers. She told them she did not care whether Jack learned the alphabet and numbers; what he needed from them was hugs.

Over time, things changed for the boy who fled hugs and rubbed off kisses. At six years old, he would sometimes race his younger sibling to sit in their mother's lap. Sometimes both youngsters would snuggle together in her lap. On school days Jack, at his initiative, and his parent would kiss good-bye at the bus stop. They did this in front of other students, who considered a kiss in public between a parent and child uncool. That year Jack was the only child getting kissed at the bus stop, but he wanted his kiss anyway.

At seven years old, Jack continued to be very demanding and very lovable. He had cut back on lap-sitting and kisses. However, he still sat, in constant motion, on his mom's lap about four times a week. Jack was popular at school and was in the advanced reading group. One memorable day I saw the boy at the bus stop. When the school bus arrived, he raced over to his mother and kissed her good-bye. Then the other students followed his example and kissed their mothers!

Jack is now eleven. He remains very demanding and very lovable. The time of bus-stop kisses is gone. However, he occasionally gives his mom a public or private bear hug. Two days ago, Jack, with a mischievous twinkle, wiped his cheek after his mother kissed him good night. The woman, assuming he was rubbing off her kiss (for the first time in several years), "threatened" to substitute a bad kiss. The boy replied playfully that he was actually <u>rubbing her kiss in</u>, to keep it longer. For Christmas he gave her a necklace that says "EXTRA SPECIAL MOM."

<u>Conclusion</u>

According to the Bible, a soft answer turneth away wrath. According to experience, a humorous response bringeth up a smile. As somebody said, "If you can't have a little fun as you go along--why go?"

So I have a thought for adoptive parents. Good humor points a child to the happy possibilities of life. Through occasional use of humor, including playfulness, you can help develop your child's sense of humor, playful spirit, and "joie de vivre"--and brighten the days for both of you.

I also have a message for adopted youngsters. As many of you learned early, life is hard. However, you can choose to smile at minor misadventures and to find fun in ordinary circumstances. To misquote the Bible and a Confucian fortune cookie, "A child who addeth humor and an upbeat attitude to his or her life's work maketh his or her own fun times!"

AUTHOR

Renée Henning is an adoptive mother and an adoptive aunt, including to young adults from Russia, Asia, and Latin America. She is also an attorney and a writer on varied subjects. Her articles have appeared in publications in North America (<u>e.g.</u>, <u>Washington Post</u>), Europe (<u>e.g.</u>, <u>Oslo Times</u>), Asia (<u>News Lens</u>), Africa (<u>e.g.</u>, <u>Modern Ghana</u>), and Oceania (<u>e.g.</u>, <u>Freelance</u>).